TESSA & SCOTT

OUR JOURNEY FROM CHILDHOOD DREAM TO GOLD

TESSA VIRTUE AND SCOTT MOIR
AS TOLD TO STEVE MILTON

TESSA
&SCOTT

OUR JOURNEY FROM CHILDHOOD DREAM TO GOLD

FOREWORD BY TRACY WILSON

ANANSI

Hardcover edition first published in Canada and the USA in 2010 by House of Anansi Press Inc.
This edition published in Canada and the USA in 2018 by House of Anansi Press Inc.
www.houseofanansi.com

House of Anansi Press is committed to protecting our natural environment.
As part of our efforts, the interior of this book is printed on paper that contains 100% post-consumer recycled fibres, is acid-free, and is processed chlorine-free.

22 21 20 19 18   1 2 3 4 5

Library and Archives Canada Cataloguing in Publication

Virtue, Tessa, author
Tessa & Scott : our journey from childhood dream to gold / Tessa Virtue and Scott Moir ; as told to Steve Milton ; foreword by Tracy Wilson. — New and expanded edition.

Issued in print and electronic formats.
ISBN 978-1-4870-0572-6 (hardcover). —ISBN 978-1-4870-0595-5 (softcover)
—ISBN 978-1-4870-0627-3 (EPUB). —ISBN 978-1-4870-0628-0 (Kindle)

1. Virtue, Tessa. 2. Moir, Scott. 3. Figure skaters — Canada — Biography.
I. Moir, Scott, author II. Milton, Steve, author III. Wilson, Tracy, writer of foreword IV. Title. V. Title: Tessa and Scott.

GV850.A2V57 2018   796.91'20922   C2018-901985-9
                          C2018-901986-7

Library of Congress Control Number: 2018940370

Text design: Gordon Sibley and Sara Loos

We acknowledge for their financial support of our publishing program
the Canada Council for the Arts, the Ontario Arts Council, and the Government of Canada.

Printed and bound in Canada

TESSA & SCOTT

To my mom, Kate, for instilling in me a sense of limitlessness. And to the B2ten crew — WE DID IT!

— T xx

For Cale and G Mac, who brought so much light into my life. I miss you both every day.

— SCOTT

Introduction

I N THE FIRST EDITION OF *TESSA AND SCOTT*, WRITTEN SHORTLY AFTER THE young Canadians won the Olympic ice dancing gold medal at Vancouver in 2010, Tessa Virtue and Scott Moir used the opportunity to shed a brighter light on many important details of their unique partnership and skating history. Much of it, Tessa says, was new information at the time.

It was their way of sharing with skating fans some of the inner workings of their career that they hadn't previously communicated, partly because they'd taken much of it for granted while living it, and partly because they were rising world-class athletes in a very competitive environment.

The same motivation — the desire to be open with loyal fans about parts of their story that weren't fully known while they were actually happening — also drives the second edition of *Tessa and Scott*. There are three new chapters, the final three of the book, picking up where the first edition left off: with Tessa and Scott formally committed only to competing in the 2011 World Championships.

But, of course, they competed for much longer than that: through the 2014 Sochi Olympics, where they won the silver medal, and, after two full seasons away from the competitive world, "the Comeback" of 2016–18 resulted in, first, an undefeated world championship season, and then culminated in their second Olympic gold in the individual ice dance event at Pyeongchang on February 20, 2018.

With their 2018 gold medals in both the team event and the individual ice dance, Tessa and Scott became the first figure skaters ever to win five Olympic medals, and just the second ice dancers to win two Olympic championships. This feat showed remarkable longevity at the summit of a sport that had been made much deeper, and more competitive, by the International Skating Union's scoring and rule changes.

And there was an almost surreal symmetry to their three individual Olympic medals, three world championships, and two world silver medals between 2010 and 2018. Each time, their main rivals — really their only rivals — were their training partners at the same club, with the same coaches. From 2010 to 2014, they trained with and competed against Meryl Davis and Charlie White of the U.S., both teams being coached in Canton, Michigan, by Marina Zoueva (and, for most of their time there, Igor Shpilband). In their two-season return, Tessa and Scott competed against France's Gabriella Papadakis and Guillaume Cizeron, both teams being coached in Montreal by Marie-France Dubreuil and Patrice Lauzon. All three couples, moreover, had been partners since they were young children.

After Vancouver 2010, Tessa and Scott were often referred to as "Canada's sweethearts," but by the time they were singing "O Canada" atop the Pyeongchang podium, they had a much wider reach. Their successful return to competition and their obvious skill, cohesion, and chemistry had magnetically attracted a following beyond Canada and even figure skating. Inside the sport, many observers, including veteran broadcasters from the United Kingdom, were comparing them favourably to Jayne Torvill and Christopher Dean, heretofore regarded as the greatest ice dancers of all time. Many thought they might even have surpassed the legendary British duo. Tessa and Scott have never made those comparisons, nor even entertained the notion that they had led an ice dancing revolution. They will only reluctantly concede that they may have "got the discussion going in a different direction," and that in advancing their sport they had benefitted from skating with and against extraordinary contemporaries, standing on the shoulders of giants both in the ice dancing world and among the Canadian skating community as a whole.

Their avalanche of titles, honours, and constructive, long-term impact on their sport are the bones of their story. But the flesh and blood, the sinews, the heart, have always been, as with most highly motivated and successful people, a little harder to see.

Their struggles at their training base in Canton, hinted at during the Sochi Olympics, were deeper than the public ever knew. Scott was enduring devastating personal losses during the second half of their undefeated 2016–17 year, the first season of "the Comeback." Twice since 2014, they have torn apart and rebuilt the basic principles of their skating. And Tessa's chronic exertional compartment syndrome threatened to derail their careers three times from 2008 to 2014.

"I think people really underestimate what it was like for Tessa," Scott says. "It changed her life for a long, long while. She couldn't walk to the store or through the park; she couldn't do anything. She was just trying to save her legs so she could get through a figure skating session."

But through it all they had each other, and learned increasingly to lean on that.

"Everyone is in love with their relationship," says Kate Virtue, Tessa's mother. "It had its up and downs but they worked every day for twenty years on that relationship. People, all of us, should learn from that."

One way to read the first edition of *Tessa and Scott* — appearing as the opening five chapters in this updated edition — is as the construction of a foundation: the bedrock of "Tessa and Scott," that essence of "them-ness" to which they would return time and time again, especially when the going got tough. It establishes their unwavering competitive nature; their differing but equally deep pools of artistic instinct, multiplied when splashed together; their commitment to art and craft, and their partnership; the core values absorbed from strong, supportive but non-meddling families; a shared passion to advance their sport beyond its traditional boundaries; and their laser-like focus on goals, over the long term and short.

Those themes remain and are amplified over the final three chapters of this second edition. But other themes also emerge. If the first edition was largely about getting to the top, the second edition is largely about what it takes to stay there. Most elite athletes will tell you that the first challenge is formidable, the second even more daunting.

The original sixth and final chapter, the bridge to the next Olympiad, has been removed and some of it rewritten into Chapter Six of the second edition. Some readers may notice a change in tone and emphasis over the final three chapters. That's to be expected, for a number of reasons. First, of course, these chapters were written eight years after the others. The concerns and focus of champions not long removed from their teens aren't quite the same as those of adult champions who are trying to retain their titles, then trying to regain them. Tessa and Scott at twenty-eight and thirty, while retaining their core personalities, are more mature and experienced than Tessa and Scott at twenty and twenty-two.

"People *should* grow and change over eight years," Scott says emphatically. "It would be sad if they didn't."

Experience is what you don't know you're gathering until you need it, so you could also consider this edition as Scott and Tessa gaining experience in the first five chapters of their astonishing career, and then applying it in the last three.

By Pyeongchang, they had learned that what mattered most to each of them was how the other felt, and the collective pursuit of the elusive sensation that derives from what you deliver in competition matching exactly what you envision and perform in practice — as they did so memorably in Pyeongchang. They repeatedly refer to it as "that feeling."

They had also learned that it was absolutely necessary to take control of their own careers, as they started to do in 2012 — partly because of Tessa's recurring leg issues — and continued more rigorously right through the final, exhilarating moments in Pyeongchang.

If you spend enough uninterrupted intimate time with Tessa and Scott deep-diving into skating and life (as I've been fortunate enough to do, twice), you are forcefully struck by how passionately interested in and fascinated by their sport they are and how captivated they are by people (those they know well as much as those they don't know at all), by the learning process, and, most of all, by each other and their nearly undefinable partnership.

They love to tell of long and theoretical discussions with their coaches, Marie-France and Patrice (who, prophetically, appear several times as role models in the first edition), about whether they'd rather have the supreme artistic moment in a program but not win, or win without having that special feeling on the ice.

"We thought we could do both," Tessa says, explaining their long pursuit of the perfect, seamless merger of artistry and athleticism.

"We still think that," Scott adds.

They also remain true to their desire for how they'd like history to regard them.

"Better that people remember us as good people than as good skaters," Tessa said in 2010, with Scott vigorously in agreement. "But if we're talking about our legacy on the ice, it would be great if people thought 'They were true dancers.' And that we made people feel something."

They will get their wish.

Steve Milton
Hamilton, Ontario
May 2018

Foreword

to the 2010 edition

BY TRACY WILSON

I WILL NEVER FORGET THE FIRST TIME I SAW TESSA VIRTUE AND SCOTT MOIR SKATE. It was at the 2003 Canadian championships, and a friend of mine said, "You have to see this new young dance team." So, on the way to a TV production meeting I told my colleagues, "Wait, there's something I have to see." Scott was fifteen years old and Tessa was just thirteen, and they were competing in their first junior national championship. You had to stand close to the boards, because if you were too far back you couldn't see them; they were both that short. As young as they were, I immediately sensed from them an innate feeling of "dance": the musicality and rhythm they both had naturally. And each of them had what is known in figure skating as wonderful edge work: where the blade appears to take off. They were skaters; they weren't playing on the drama.

Even as junior skaters, I could see that both Tessa and Scott had that perfect balance between athlete and artist. As they matured, refined their training, and gathered more experience, that balance became even more evident.

Dance is about making it look easy, but the skill and technique has to be there first. Otherwise it's just fluff, and it shows. As an ice dancer, that's one of my biases: there's a physical, athletic side to the sport and it's absolutely essential. To me, the most important relationship in all skating is the one between the blade and the ice. And the second most important is the body to the music. If you start with these two elements, everything builds on them. That's what takes it to the next level. Jayne Torvill and Christopher Dean had it. And so do Tessa and Scott. They are pure dancers.

As a spectator, you may not understand what it is but you know that you love it. It's the pure technique, the heart of the art. That pure technique, that heart, is part of how Tessa and Scott transcend our sport more than most figure skaters ever have. Another part of transcending the sport is their universal appeal. Tessa and Scott attract everyone. An athlete can watch and appreciate the athleticism and be drawn to them. An artist can watch the beautiful shapes and be drawn to them. A musician will be drawn to them because of the sheer musicality of their work. They have something for everyone, just as Ekaterina Gordeeva and Sergei Grinkov — the greatest pairs team of our time—did.

Tessa and Scott's skating is ethereal: they take you to a higher place.

While it is Tessa and Scott who actually go out and do it, a pillar of their success is who they've found to work with over their careers. Every conceivable thing has been taken care of, every detail seen to. Marina Zoueva has the vision and wisdom to know what brilliance looks like and how to best reveal it. Igor Shpilband's technical training is, arguably, the best in the world. Marina and Igor both do choreography and technical training, but together they bring balance. And it was evident when I first saw Tessa and Scott as juniors that they had already been properly and precisely trained by, first, Carol Moir, then Paul MacIntosh and Suzanne Killing. They have such great knees, edges, and blades.

And most importantly, as people Tessa and Scott are so easy to like. They're open and they both care so much about everyone else. Watching them skate, you can see their good-to-the-bone strong character. Everything they do is for the right reasons. I went to Ilderton for their homecoming celebration, and when you see where they come from, you can understand their strength. It's based in the community and in their families. And their community becomes their family. That's their foundation, and I think it is how they were able to withstand the kind of pressure they faced in their Olympic season and with Tessa's terrible shin injuries, which were a lot worse and lasted a lot longer than anyone outside their coaches and family realized.

Much is made of Tessa and Scott becoming the first Canadians, and first North Americans, to win the Olympic ice dancing gold medal. And, it was an important milestone because in the past, political and regional biases often influenced the outcome. It was so great for the sport of ice dance to see the best team on the night win.

Their free dance will go down as one of the all-time best Olympic performances. In an often controversial judged sport such as ice dance, Tessa and Scott silenced the critics, they took the sport to a new level, and one can only watch in awe and wonder at where they may take it in the future.

Tracy Wilson
Olympic Ice Dancing Bronze Medallist
Toronto, Ontario
August 2010

"I WASN'T GOOD
UNTIL I STARTED
SKATING WITH TESSA.
THE COMPETITIVENESS
REALLY PUSHED ME." —*Scott*

Chapter One

THE EARLY YEARS

During their first year together
Tessa and Scott forged what would become an
extraordinary ice dancing partnership.

THE FINAL JOYOUS STRAINS OF "O CANADA" still hung in the air when the roar began ripping through the arena like indoor thunder. Nearly 12,000 people, all of them on their feet, many of them still dabbing away at involuntary tears, had barely finished wailing ". . . on guard for thee!" before shifting seamlessly into yet another deafening ovation for the young woman and man on the top step of the podium.

Scott Moir pushed the flower bouquet in his left hand straight upward in celebration. Tessa Virtue hoisted the bouquet in her right. With his right hand he thrust the huge, thick gold medal away from his body toward the bellowing audience. With her left hand she subtly touched the medal dangling from her neck, almost as if she were making sure it was still there. Pure elation was written in bold letters across their faces and their bodies occasionally twitched in uncontrolled happiness. Head to toe, they visibly throbbed with joy. For the better part of an hour, bedlam and unabashed national pride had engulfed the Pacific Coliseum. The clapping and the cheering and the crying had begun partway through Tessa and Scott's brilliantly uplifting interpretation of Mahler's 5th Symphony.

It reached a crescendo as she stretched across his lap in their finishing position, his right cheek pressed against her left, their eyes squeezed shut and Scott whispering, "Thank you so much."

While they stood on the podium, after wisely letting the roars of the crowd speak alone for a few moments, veteran CTV commentator Rod Black interjected, "Only in your dreams — sometimes — does something this sweet ever happen!"

In the BBC broadcast booth, skating legend Robin Cousins told his viewers in Great Britain that the young Canadians were the only couple who could ever make him temporarily forget Jayne Torvill and Christopher Dean, fellow Britons who were considered the greatest ice dancers who ever lived.

In the vast media centre, scores of journalists hunched over their laptops hammering out their stories on deadline, trying to capture the beauty of the mood piece they had just witnessed, and recounting the seemingly mercurial rise of the youngest ice dancers, and the first from North America, ever to win the Olympics.

But only Tessa and Scott, and their families, really knew how long and difficult their journey had been, and how the most important part of it was that they had travelled it . . . together.

Opposite: Tessa Virtue and Scott Moir, gold medallists in ice dance at the Winter Olympics in Vancouver, B.C., February 2010.

TURNING NORTH OFF MIDDLESEX COUNTY Road 16 and into the Ilderton Fairgrounds, a visitor is immediately struck by two dominating images. The first is the space. The grounds, officially only 6.31 acres, spill into a horizon of rich, rolling farm fields, creating the sense of endless room. Room to breathe, room to play, and, most importantly, room to grow. The second is the big blue front wall of the Ilderton Arena and Curling Club, located only a few steps off the village's main road, directly behind the compact memorial to local war heroes. Like Vancouver's Pacific Coliseum, the site of the 2010 Olympic figure skating competition, it is the centrepiece of a vast community meeting ground, and, like the Coliseum, it is renowned for its annual exhibition and fair.

IT IS THE KIND OF PLACE WHERE YOU DON'T LOCK YOUR CAR IN THE ARENA PARKING LOT. AND IT IS THE KIND OF PLACE WHERE A BUSY LONDON FAMILY WOULD GLADLY TAKE THEIR SIX-YEAR-OLD DAUGHTER TO LEARN HOW TO FIGURE SKATE.

The Ilderton Arena, constructed in the early 1970s to replace the old Quonset hut rink, overshadows the smaller community centre, adjacent Legion Hall, and original arena, just to the west, and the exhibition hall, livestock stalls, and meticulously maintained show corrals to the north. Its outer walls — both the cinder-block lower half and the corrugated metal-siding upper half — are a distinctive and imposing dark blue, which, with its location close to the main road, makes the functional building seem bigger than it actually is.

The arena is the absolute hub of cultural life in the village. Ilderton, with three new subdivisions, has nearly doubled its population to about 2,000 residents in the last twenty-five years, but is still markedly rural. It offers the best of both worlds: the classic charm and friendliness of small-town life and the urban amenities of London, the largest city in southwest Ontario, just a ten-minute drive down County Road 20. It is the kind of place where you don't lock your car in the arena parking lot. And it is the kind of place where a busy London family would gladly take their six-year-old daughter to learn how to figure skate.

"It had such a great reputation," says Kate Virtue, whose two daughters, ten-year-old Jordan and six-year-old Tessa arrived at the Ilderton Arena in the fall of 1995. "And there was a bit of hurry to it."

Tessa's grade one class at Stoneybrook Public School in North London was scheduled for a skating outing later in the fall, and Tessa wanted to make sure she could skate well before then. "That's typical of her personality," Kate says.

Indeed, Tessa was, and still is, an extremely competitive and determined soul. She is the youngest of Kate and Jim Virtue's four children, who range widely in age. When Tessa unsuspectingly began what would be a fourteen-year odyssey to the top of the figure skating world, Kate and Jim had a child in grade one, grade five (Jordan), grade nine (Kevin), and first-year university (Casey).

Kate, a Registrar of The Law Society of Upper Canada, had studied ballet when she was young, and Jim, a lawyer, excelled at a number of sports. Their children reflected those interests and skills, engaging in a plethora of activities. Tessa began studying ballet and modern dance at Errington Graham Dance when she was three and moved to Swan Studio Dance at age six; she and Jordan also took high-level competitive gymnastics and played soccer; their older brothers played high-level hockey and football (both were quarterbacks); and Kevin was such a talented baseball player that he got a scholarship to a college in Texas and was drafted by the Baltimore Orioles. The family was busy with somebody's activities, or several of them, almost every night. Before she came to Ilderton for formal instruction, Tessa's skating experience consisted of shuffling around local London rinks "on Canadian

Above: Tessa, age 6.
Left: An early skating lesson, age 3½.
Below: The Virtue family: *(left to right)*
Kevin, Kate, Tessa, Jim, Jordan, and Casey.

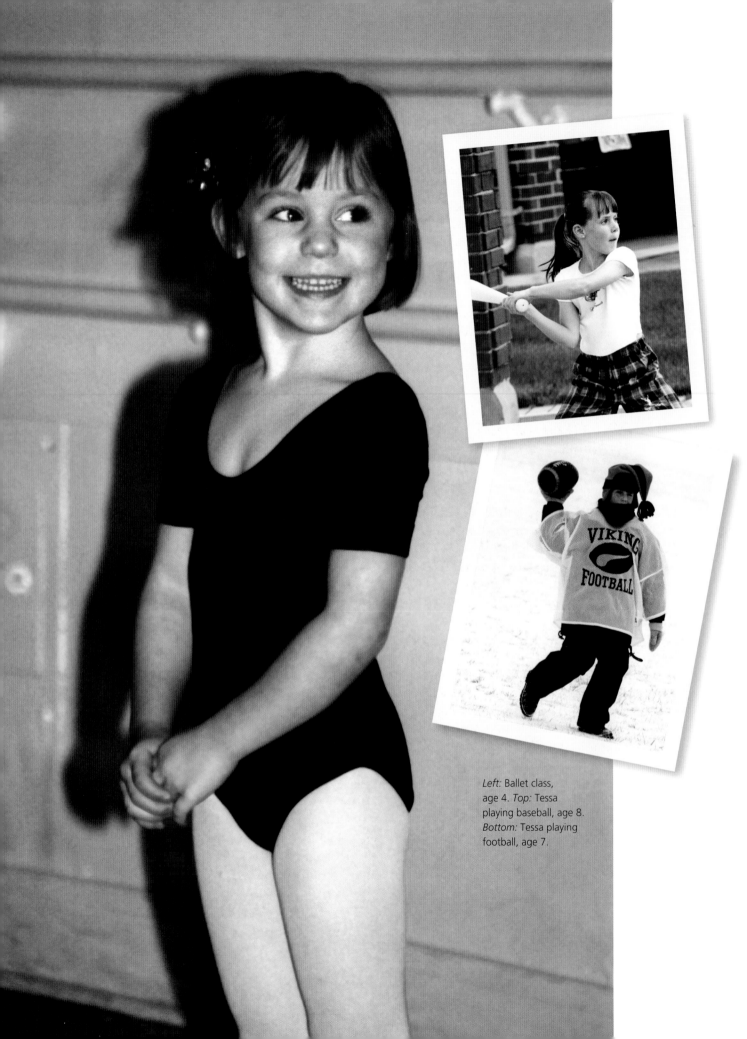

Left: Ballet class, age 4. *Top:* Tessa playing baseball, age 8. *Bottom:* Tessa playing football, age 7.

Tire plastic skates" and getting rudimentary lessons from Kevin, when older brother and baby sister would grab some time together on the ice surface prior to his AAA hockey games. "As a kid I was a bruiser," Tessa recalls. "I grew up with two older brothers and an older sister, and played bodycheck hockey games and mini-sticks. When I was little, while watching my brothers play football, I was cheerleading on the sidelines, doing my gymnastics routines. I was always active. I was a bit of a tomboy. I was a tough kid."

Tumbling about with her much older siblings, trying to keep up despite their superior size and strength, helped fill the deep well of compet-

those first few days at Ilderton. "I couldn't make it around the ice. It's so funny to go back now, because it's really the tiniest little ice surface. But back then I couldn't even see over the boards. It was intimidating, because there were so many people. And I had my little helmet on." And her great big gloves on. She was small and got cold easily, so she wore huge warm mitts, prompting Danny Moir to nickname her "Big Hands."

Danny Moir and his first cousin Sheri Moir were the stars of the Ilderton Figure Skating Club. A talented team working their way up the ice dancing ladder, which in those days was a slow and very political process, they would eventually

"AS A KID I WAS A BRUISER, I GREW UP WITH TWO OLDER BROTHERS AND AN OLDER SISTER, AND PLAYED BODYCHECK HOCKEY GAMES AND MINI-STICKS." — *Tessa*

itiveness inside of Tessa Virtue. Her mother says that she wasn't as overtly competitive as her brothers and sister, but that she "had resolve."

"I'm pretty reserved and I guess I'm shy until you get to know me. But when I get down to any activity, school too, I'm kind of a perfectionist," Tessa explains. "I see that trait in my siblings as well. And my parents are both that way, so I think it's just a part of me."

Modern dance and ballet were her first loves. But she was interested in many things, and pursued sport, piano lessons, and elementary school with the same committed drive. She always had a goal, and would pursue it relentlessly. She recalls being in the CanSkate program — a series of progressive learn-to-skate lessons administered by Skate Canada, the country's umbrella organization for figure skating — lined up in rows with her peers doing elementary exercises on one side of the Ilderton rink. But she soon noticed that the advanced class on the other side of the rink was learning far more interesting things, and was determined to get there as soon as she could. And, to one of the smallest kids on the ice, the other side was a long way away.

"Oh, it seemed huge!" she remembers of

become the 1999 national novice champions and the 2001 national junior silver medallists. They trained in Kitchener-Waterloo with their coach, Paul MacIntosh, who is affectionately called "Mr. Mac," but the pair also skated regularly in Ilderton.

The Moirs were the dominant family in the Ilderton skating community. Carol and Alma MacCormack, twin sisters who moved with their army family from Ottawa to London during their teens, were good age-class figure skaters themselves and eventually became coaches. Alma travelled a four-town circuit in southern Ontario before settling into the Ilderton Club with Carol in 1983. The sisters were among the main reasons the small rink enjoyed such a big reputation and became the largest club in the London area.

Alma married Joe Moir, who grew up on the family farm on the same road as the Ilderton Arena, about four concessions to the east. Carol married Joe's older brother Paul. While Carol and Paul had three girls, Alma and Joe had three boys: Danny (born in 1980), Charlie (born in 1984), and Scott (born September 2, 1987). Scott, like his future partner, was the youngest of a rambunctious athletic bunch.

Left: Scott's baptism, October 1987.
Below: The Moir boys: *(top to bottom)* Danny, Charlie, and Scott in 1988.

Just after Danny was born, Alma and Joe Moir moved into a two-storey home on Ilderton Road, also known as County Road 16. To the south, there are expansive farm fields. A few doors to the west, more vast agricultural acreage. But along the east side of the Moir property runs a short driveway that leads directly to the Legion Hall and community centre, just a few metres behind the Moirs' backyard. About fifty metres across the parking lot looms what Scott calls "the beautiful blue" of the Ilderton Arena.

"I don't think Scott understood that not everyone grows up with an arena in their backyard," laughs Paul MacIntosh, the well-respected dance coach from Waterloo.

Because skating was front and centre in his family, Scott doesn't really remember it not being a part of his life. Like his older brothers, he lived for hockey, and his early figure skating training was a way to improve his individual skills for the team game.

"I got put into both. My mom was a pro at the skating club, so obviously I was going to do that," he says. "If there was a CanSkate session, I might as well be on the ice trying to do it. But unlike Tessa, I had no concept of anybody getting better. When I got on, I pretty much just wanted to cause as much trouble as I could before the hour was up. I would just skate as fast as I could. I didn't care who was around me and didn't really listen to the program assistants. My mom and my aunt were in charge and I think I knew — a little bit more than they thought I did — that I could get away with a lot."

To keep home and work as separate as possible, Carol and Alma had agreed to coach each other's children. And Carol loved coaching her youngest nephew.

"For Scott and his brothers, figure skating was their second sport, hockey was the first," Carol said. "They were doing it to become better skaters for hockey. Scotty was very energetic, never standing still, and full of charisma. I could have coached him all day, he had so much energy and he made us all laugh."

Scott's ability to make people (including himself) laugh, to put them at ease, was not only important to a coach at the end of a long, tiring day, it would serve Scott well later in life when things began to get tense, as they always do at the highest levels of competitive skating.

"He's always been a little bit of a character, all three of the boys are," Alma says. "He's a good mix of our oldest two. Charlie's probably the funniest but also the quietest. Danny is easy to get to know. We always got compliments on how he talked to adults. He was always out there, while Charlie was a bit more reserved. Scott's the youngest, so maybe he needed to show off to get attention. We don't have pictures of him being serious; he always has a great smile on his face."

Scott took his earliest figure skating lessons in hockey skates, as many of the boys in Ilderton did.

Clockwise:
Joe and Scott, summer 1988; Scott in "Country Bear Jambouree," age 4; Scott's kindergarten photo, 1992–93; Danny, Charlie, and Scott, 1990.
Centre: Scott, 18 months.

But when he was six and starting to learn elementary toe jumps, he needed figure skates with their toe picks. He got two pairs of hand-me-downs from one of his cousins, but they were white. One pair the family painted black, and the other required black boot covers to hide the original colour.

"One time, my mom had forgotten to put one boot cover on," he says. "I can remember one of the rink guys saying 'nice white skates' so I wouldn't go on the ice. I had one white skate, and one black skate, and I thought the world was going to figure out that the black skate was actually a white skate too. White skates were supposed to be for girls."

At the time, Scott was playing a great deal of hockey for Ilderton teams, one year in a more local league against other teams from small towns, the next in AAA, the highest level in Ontario minor hockey. He admits that he far preferred hockey to skating — he played at a high level until his early teens — and would often cry and hide in his room when his father said it was time to make the short walk to the arena for figure skating practice. Once he got to the rink, however, he was enthusiastic.

"I never compared the two sports when I was young, they were completely different," he says. "The figure skating always made my hockey better, but when I played hockey and came back to figure skating it just made it a lot worse. I would bend over again and I would hit my toe picks a couple of times. My buddies always said that when I played hockey they could tell I was a figure skater, because I had a good back and good posture."

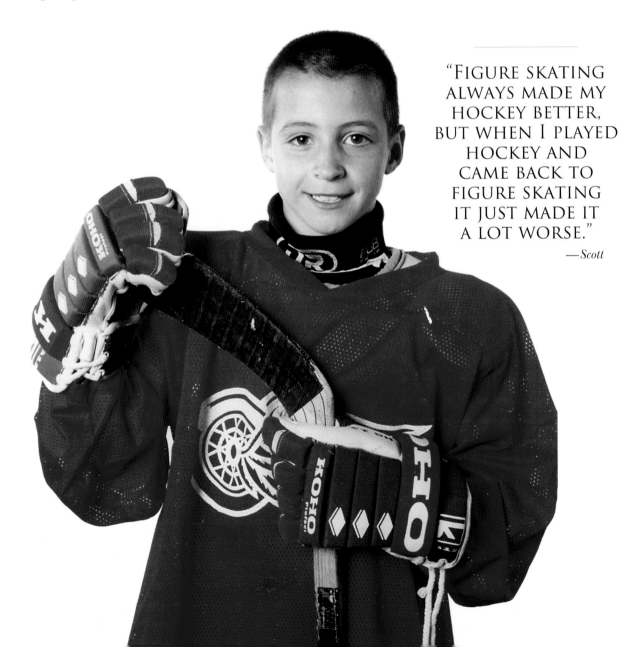

"FIGURE SKATING ALWAYS MADE MY HOCKEY BETTER, BUT WHEN I PLAYED HOCKEY AND CAME BACK TO FIGURE SKATING IT JUST MADE IT A LOT WORSE."
—*Scott*

When Tessa started skating in Ilderton, Scott had just turned eight, had already done his first solo, *Sesame Street Rock*, and had taken a liking to the jumps. To lighten the load on a very active family with two working parents, Kate Virtue's mother, Eleanor, often drove Tessa the fifteen or twenty minutes from the Virtue family home near the University of Western Ontario to Ilderton once or twice a week for her skating lessons. One incident from that first winter not only rings with irony, given where Tessa eventually went with skating, it hints at the source of Tessa's lifelong love of fashion.

"Scott's aunt, Carol, was my singles coach," Tessa says, "and one day she said, 'We're going to sign her up for Test Day,'" [a day when skaters are evaluated against Skate Canada standards] "but my grandma said, 'No, no, no, we're not taking this seriously. No tests, no competitions, this is just for fun,' because I was doing so many other sports, was serious about gymnastics, and was very competitive. Then my mom heard that Test Day might be an opportunity to buy a dress, so she signed me up."

While Tessa and Scott were nearly oblivious to each other's presence over Tessa's first two winters at the rink, their mothers weren't.

"I do remember seeing Scott," Kate Virtue says. "He was dancing with another little girl at the time. You could pick the Moir kids out by the way they skated. They were the best in the rink. He was adorable and he had kind of an impishness to him."

And Alma Moir had noticed Tessa: "She always wore these big mitts. And she had the gymnastic body, the dance training, and the dancer's back."

Carol Moir, who was teaching both of them singles skating, says Tessa was "a very petite athlete. Freckle-faced and pigtailed. Very cute. She was very small but very athletic. And she was always very mature for her age. She was athletically developed so I always had to remind myself 'this girl is only seven years old.'"

Neither Scott nor Tessa remembers the specific moment they met, comparing it to school where "you just sort of realize you know somebody," but they do remember becoming much more familiar with each other during the summer camps at the arena.

Opposite: Scott's hockey photo from Mid-Elgin Red Wings team.
Above right: Tessa with her grandmother Eleanor.
Above left: Skating carnival, March 1996.
Right: Tessa at age 7.

"He had a buzzed head," Tessa says.

"It was summer, man, it was a buzz cut," Scott replies.

"Sometimes you'd dye it blond."

"Yeah, I did a whole bunch of things to it."

The camp, which provided an all-day program of swimming, crafts, gym, ballet, karate, and figure skating, was called MAC, an acronym for Marg, Alma, and Carol, the three coaching sisters. Later, they realized that MAC was also the nickname of their father, Irven MacCormack.

"We were in all the same classes together," Scott continues. "I was getting kicked out of the ballet classes, because I was just goofing around. We were by far the youngest in our group. We were pretty good, and everybody else was probably in seventh or eighth grade."

Tessa says of those first two summers, "I don't remember necessarily a first attraction but I remember always sort of being aware of where Scott

was in the rink. He never stayed in one spot. In any activity group he was kind of buzzing about, but I was always keeping an eye on him for some reason."

Generally, though, like most kids of that age, skaters at the camp were less interested in what individuals were doing than what groups were up to, particularly the pranks.

"One time the girls took all the boys' skating clothes and replaced them with spandex skirts," Tessa laughs. "And the guys wore them on the ice."

The boys came up with a plan to pay the girls back, but it didn't have quite the intended result.

"We wanted to put chickens in their dressing room," Scott says. "But we couldn't get any chickens at that time of year, so we got little chicks instead and the girls all went 'Awwww, they're so cute!' They wanted to take them home."

Among the other campers were Scott's brother Charlie, his cousins, and Tessa's older sister, Jordan.

"My brother would constantly play tricks on me," Scott says, with great respect for Charlie's creativity. "He'd say, 'Let's play hide-and-seek, because we don't want to go to dance class.' So I'd walk into the dance class forty minutes late because I'd been hiding in the closet. And my brother had been sitting there the whole time."

Foreshadowing a deeper relationship between the families, the Moir and Virtue kids all got along, and Cara Moir and Jordan Virtue became good friends. In fact, they played a major, if unforeseen, role in creating one of the greatest partnerships in Canadian skating history.

"My sister and Scott's cousin decided it would be kind of cute if we were 'dating,'" Tessa says. "And I liked Scott. I don't know if he liked me, but we just went along with it."

"Were we not the hot topic by week four, though?" Scott asks rhetorically. "We were the big new couple on campus. We 'dated' for eight months. Why do I remember that? Because eight months is a long time for eight and ten years old. We probably only had two phone conversations and I remember my brothers talking me through the phone call with her, I was so nervous. We'd sit there and not say anything. It was a cool thing to do: phone and talk to each other."

Left: (left to right) Scott, Charlie, Danny, Sheri Moir (cousin), Tessa, Leanne Moir (cousin), and Jordan. *Below: (top to bottom)* Danny, Charlie, and Scott, skating carnival 1998.

"My sister and Scott's cousin decided it would be kind of cute if we were 'dating,' and I liked Scott. I don't know if he liked me, but we just went along with it." — *Tessa*

"Dating" was a little strong. It was the summer of 1997, and heading into grades three and five they were too young for even puppy love, so it was just a label that others attached to them, mostly for their own amusement.

Tessa talked about Scott during school hours at Stoneybrook Public School, but when Scott's friends at Oxbow Public School found out about Tessa, he somehow felt he had to "end" it. His friends called Tessa and quickly handed the phone back to Scott, who blurted, "I don't want to go out with you any more," then hung up.

And although for the next dozen years every reporter and skating fan, and eventually, millions of TV viewers, tried to link them as boyfriend and girlfriend, that has been the extent of their romantic history.

"But, after we got over our little relationship thing, we were actually able to talk more," Scott says. "And our relationship grew."

Tessa always wondered whether Jordan and Cara talking about her and Scott "dating" had any influence on Cara's mother pairing the two together.

"They have to take the blame, or I guess I should say the credit," Carol Moir says. "Scott had a former dance partner, for two months leading to a local competition the previous winter, and she had decided she didn't want to do it any more. That fall I was thinking, 'I've got to find Scott another partner.' And then Tessa skated by. Cara and Jordan had already put them together, and Tessa was the right size and the proper skill level for Scott. And the families got along well, and that's very important in partnerships."

Tessa had only just started grade three but says, "one thing I do remember vividly was Carol calling me over — Scott was standing with her — and just getting me to stand beside Scott to see height-wise how we matched. I remember standing there and not knowing what she had in mind and not even thinking this would be a partnership

Tessa and Scott, 1998.

thing. I just remember thinking, 'Why are we comparing heights here?' It was in front of the window in the corner. I can picture it so vividly. Then she had us skate perimeter, where you just skate left-right-left-right."

"We did not get it the first time," Scott says, picking up the story. "We kept hitting each other in the perimeter. Then we did a couple of exercises in the dance position, and that was a lot of work for the first day. I think I was thinking, 'When can I go and skate by myself?' You're so shy at that age. I remember being so nervous holding her hand, even though she had these huge mitts on. I was just so nervous, we were probably barely touching each other. I just wanted it to be over."

Neither the eight-year-old nor the ten-year-old had any clue from that first shaky foray that they were headed for a full-time partnership. In fact Tessa, who had been partnered for a few instructional dances with Scott's older brother, had written in her grade one notebook that her dream was to go to the Olympics "with DANNY Moir."

Above: With coach
Carol Moir in 1998.
Left: Tessa solo, 1997.

Both Tessa and Scott demonstrated skating skills beyond their years and each reached the Western Ontario sectionals (the first of two steps toward the national championships) in singles, which is an accomplishment given the number of skaters in the region.

Tessa was the first and only skater Carol Moir ever taught who mastered a single Axel in one lesson. She loved to skate fast, and loved doing spiral after spiral in front of the arena window. "And I suppose that even at that age I was kind of a performer," she says. According to those closest to her, whenever she skated, even at the youngest age and perhaps from her dance training, she had the poise and projection to capture every pair of eyes in the arena.

"I loved doing double jumps, but when it came to starting a double Axel or a triple jump, I didn't really want to do it," Tessa says. "I wasn't scared. I just liked landing things. As I said, I'm a perfectionist."

Because they had always been the smallest and youngest, growing up with older siblings, taking classes with older skaters, playing hockey or competing in gymnastics against older athletes, and having friends who were older, Tessa and Scott were always trying to keep up. So at the time Tessa hadn't realized she had become a very good skater, Scott hadn't realized he had become a very good skater, and neither knew that they were already showing a germ of promise as a dance couple. Carol had talked to both sets of parents about it, and Tessa and Scott were soon skating almost exclusively with each other during dance sessions, thereby forming an unspoken partnership.

"We were so young that we just kept doing what we were told," Scott recalls. "I wasn't good until I started skating with Tessa. As she says, the competitiveness really pushed me. Before, I didn't care. Once I was skating with Tessa, she would do something and I would say to myself, 'I guess I'd better learn how to do that better than her or else it's going to look like this girl's beating me.' That was a lot of what motivated me."

"And in our singles, when we weren't skating together," Tessa continues, "it was, 'Oh, he's doing his double toe. I'm going to do MY double toe.'"

Even at their first summer camp together they were competitive at the ping-pong table. (A memory that would come back to Scott more than a dozen years later, watching Sidney Crosby and his teammates wage spirited table tennis tournaments in the Olympic Village. Tessa wasn't able to spend a lot of time in the athlete's lounge because of

> "I LOVED DOING DOUBLE JUMPS, BUT WHEN IT CAME TO STARTING A DOUBLE AXEL OR A TRIPLE JUMP, I DIDN'T REALLY WANT TO DO IT, I WASN'T SCARED. I JUST LIKED LANDING THINGS. AS I SAID, I'M A PERFECTIONIST." — *Tessa*

extensive physiotherapy sessions, but she recalls that they also played a lot of bubble hockey in her basement when they were kids. Tessa points out that she can still beat Scott when they play on the bubble hockey game at the rink when they need a diversion from training. To which Scott jokingly replies, "Tessa is stretching this, she can't beat me at bubble hockey.")

That doubly fuelled competitiveness was tempered nicely by the attitude that the Moirs in general, and Scott in particular, brought to the sport. They were expected to practise diligently, and compete to the best of their ability. "But we always had fun with it too," Scott explains. "We were always a pretty easygoing family, and we knew it wasn't really that important to win the home-region championships. So if something went wrong, we just kind of laughed it off. And we always made jokes at each other. There were always six of us there competing. Six Moirs. We knew if you had a really bad program, you could always look up in the stands and they'd all be there laughing at you anyways."

Tessa remembers watching Scott in a local singles competition when he was about ten years old. "He was about to skate to his "Lone Ranger" program and was nervous about going on. His

"I WAS TEN YEARS OLD, I DIDN'T HAVE
THE ALLOWANCE TO BUY FLOWERS.
I KISSED HER ON THE CHEEK THAT NIGHT
TOO. SHE HAD TO BE IN THE NEXT NUMBER
RIGHT AWAY SO IT PROBABLY WASN'T
THE BEST TIME." — *Scott*

cousin Leanne, I think trying to relax him, said, 'Okay, Scott, do a back flip. He was doing a backwards shoot-the-duck and was supposed to get up and go into a single Lutz jump. But instead he did a back roll on the ice and just kept going. His face did not change a bit. He was straight-faced, and looked almost disinterested. I remember vividly, sitting in the stands with his mom, and she was laughing!"

It was clear to the grown-ups around them that through these shared experiences, their rapidly escalating skating skills, and their innate matched competitiveness, Tessa and Scott were becoming uncommonly close friends, even if they couldn't recognize it themselves.

PAUL MACINTOSH WAS VISITING ILDERTON ONCE a week to coach Danny and Sheri Moir, his rising ice dance team, and it was natural that he would watch another Moir and his new partner and sometimes work with them. He recalls seeing Tessa and Scott in the first year of their partnership. "Scott likes to play down the relationship they had when they were young, but even as young people they seemed to beat with one heart," Paul says. "They had an uncanny sense of unison. And there was a sense of something in their ankles and knees that told you they had musicality and a sense of rhythm. Once in a lifetime you get kids like that."

What Scott saw as "doing what we were told" his coaches saw as one of the most important assets in individual sport: coachability. Carol Moir identified it in both kids right away, and all the coaches they would encounter in the future would be grateful for the young team's willingness to quickly grasp instructions and then follow them, no matter what they might have thought about those instructions.

While much of that was native to their individual personalities, some of it was clearly born in the safety and comfort of an arena where maximum effort was expected but where it was okay, and sometimes worth laughing about, to make an honest mistake. And where the coaches enjoyed your complete trust because not only were they skilled and perceptive, they were friends and family.

Tessa and Scott's partnership through most of that initial year together (and Tessa's second winter at the rink) consisted mainly of skating together to the four dances that would be played on the arena sound system during group training sessions.

"I knew we were kind of partners," Scott recalls. "When Tessa was on the ice I'd think 'Oh, we're going to have to skate together today.' That kind of thing. It was sorta cool, but very nerve-racking to be skating with a girl and holding hands. I liked Tessa. But I was just kind of cruising around. I still really wanted to be a singles skater. It just happened one day that we were together."

By the time the Ilderton Skating Carnival, the highlight of the local skating calendar, rolled round in April 1998, Tessa and Scott were in a loosely knit partnership. But during the carnival they performed only as singles skaters. It was during their "dating" phase, and both were portraying acrobats, once again triggering the mutual competitiveness that fuelled their skating.

"You gave me flowers," says Tessa, giggling. "But I was going to get them anyways. You just happened to grab them from the bucket and give them to me."

"I was ten years old," Scott retorts. "I didn't have the allowance to buy flowers. I kissed her on the cheek that night too. She had to be in the next num-

W.O.S. Fall Invitational
1998

Tessa & Scott

Opposite: Presenting flowers at Ilderton Carnival, 1998.
Above: A Polaroid from the Western Ontario Section Invitational.
Right: Tessa and Scott, 1999. *Below:* Scott's grade school photo.

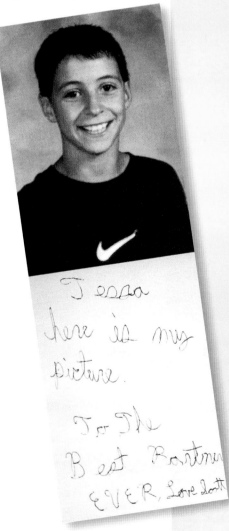

Tessa
here is my
picture.

To The
Best Partner
EVER, Love Scott

ber right away so it probably wasn't the best time."

That winter, Carol Moir suggested to Tessa and Scott that they enter a Western Ontario Section invitational event where they would be required to perform a swing dance. "In order to motivate us to actually work, you throw a competition in there, or a test," Scott theorizes, but this particular duo needed far less motivation to work than anyone their age, or much older.

At the event, both sets of parents were standing together on the wooden steps of the arena, laughing because their children "looked so cute" together, Kate Virtue recalls. "But we couldn't let the kids see us laughing. Tessa was wearing one of Sheri's skating dresses which was missing a few beads, which bothered Tessa. Then Alma said, laughing. 'Oh, he's doing the wrong steps!' Scott had forgotten his steps."

Nobody can remember where they finished in that event, but what emerged from their debut competition together was perhaps the first ritual, and certainly an early pillar, of their relationship. From that point on, Tessa always learned both her own and Scott's steps for every competitive program. "He's always forgotten his," Tessa says. "From the beginning I learned that if I made a mental note of his steps, then I'd be able to help him a little bit." It was an early signpost of the give-and-take required to sustain a long-term partnership, although neither was thinking of it that way at the time.

During the spring skating school after the 1998 carnival, Tessa and Scott found themselves training more and more often together, and there was a formal acknowledgement of their partnership. Joe, Alma, and Scott Moir and Jim, Kate, and Tessa Virtue began what would become their annual spring meeting to make sure the kids wanted to commit to another season of lessons and training. By mutual agreement, it was to be a year-to-year process.

"With Tessa and Scott, we'd take it one year at time," Carol Moir adds. "If Tessa took after her dad and grew tall and Scott didn't, they'd both have to move on to other partners."

While Tessa did have a growth spurt and Scott's came later on, through most of their career they have been close to the same height. It's one of the traits that skating people always notice when seeing them for the first time.

As the 1997–98 season drew to a close, Carol Moir considered it a "really fun first year together." Tessa and Scott had evolved, rather than jumped, into an ice dance partnership. "It was never a conscious decision for either of us to say, 'Okay, I'm going to go the dance route,'" Tessa says. "Or even 'I want to be a figure skater.' I never said that, or really had a chance to decide that. It just kept going."

"I always think that dance kind of chose us," Scott continues. "There's no doubt that we enjoyed doing it. We were pretty young, but we always had a lot of fun with it. It was kind of exciting, and the ball just never stopped rolling."

But wider input would be needed to keep that ball rolling. They might have arrived at ice dancing almost accidentally, but underneath Scott's serial playfulness and Tessa's outsized sophistication they were both unusually determined and competitive kids and were already thinking about becoming the best they could be, probably with the Olympics swimming subconsciously around in their minds. And no matter how well Carol Moir had constructed those first physical and psychological steps, for Tessa and Scott to climb the ice dance ladder — the most hierarchical in all of figure skating — their coach knew they would eventually have to look beyond the big beautiful blue of Ilderton.

"I ALWAYS THINK THAT DANCE KIND OF CHOSE US."

—*Scott*

Opposite and above:
Tessa and Scott
during the first year
of their partnership.

"THEY HAD A
MUSICALITY
THAT WAS DIFFERENT
THAN ANY OTHER KIDS
I HAD EVER TAUGHT.
IT WASN'T JUST THE
(TIME) COUNT,
IT WAS THE CHARACTER
AND THE WAY THEY
PLAYED OFF
EACH OTHER." —*Suzanne Killing-Wood*

Chapter Two

COMPETITIVE EDGE

AN UNEXPECTED CHAMPIONSHIP WIN
PROMPTED THE FIRST INKLING THAT SOMETHING SPECIAL
WAS ON THE HORIZON FOR TESSA AND SCOTT.

"IT WAS A NATURAL," CAROL MOIR SAYS, THAT Tessa and Scott should start gradually working with Paul MacIntosh, who had taught all levels of skating and was respected for elevating promising skaters into international athletes. "Mr. Mac" was already coaching Scott's oldest brother, Danny, and Carol's middle daughter, Sheri, in Kitchener-Waterloo, where, Carol says, "They had ice five days a week, and in our little arena we got only three days of skating a week."

So, in the summer of 1998, less than a year after they had stood side-by-side comparing heights in front of the window in the Ilderton Arena, Tessa and Scott began travelling the 100 kilometres to Kitchener once a week to take lessons from Paul and his young assistant Suzanne Killing. They continued those trips, once or twice per week, through the school year — Tessa was in grade four at Stoneybrook Public School in London, Scott in grade six at Oxbow Public School in Ilderton — and as they became more and more immersed in ice dance and their partnership, they steadily increased the frequency. By the 1999–2000 season they were making the hour-long commute three or four, and sometimes five, mornings a week, and they soon began devoting parts of their summers to living and training in Waterloo. Carol continued to teach them their singles lessons and, in regular communication with Mr. Mac, would assist with

Opposite: At Tomorrow's Champions Competition, 2000. *Above:* Tessa and Scott at a training session during the 1999–2000 season.

their dance steps and programs whenever they were on the ice at Ilderton Arena.

"We would meet at 4:45 or 5 a.m. at the Bethel Church on Ilderton Road," Tessa recalls. "That church was a big part of our childhood because that's where we'd spend so much time waiting for each other. We'd switch cars to whichever parent was driving us that day. Then we'd fall asleep right away. And we'd wake up just before we got to the rink. Then, after we skated, we'd get a hot chocolate, drive back, and change cars again at

Bethel Church or we'd be dropped off at school."

That was a time and energy expenditure far beyond what other children their age could conceive of, but Tessa and Scott had already become dedicated to their sport and to each other. And in that summer of 1998, Tessa dramatically put words and action to that commitment.

To this day, despite how much Tessa loves skating, ballet and modern dance — "dance, period" — are still her deepest passions. "I was always choreographing dances off the ice, even hip-hop," she says. She continued to take ballet lessons from Jennifer Swan in London and was part of a London company called Children's Dance Project, performing recitals around the city. Later, she went to classes at Kitchener's Carousel Dance Studios two or three times a week.

Tessa cut skating camp short in the summer of 1998, because she had auditioned for the National Ballet School in Toronto and wanted to spend July in the school's summer program. It was an incredibly intense month and for the first two weeks, the students were not allowed to have any contact with friends or family.

Opposite: Tessa and Scott during the 1999–2000 season.
Above: At the rink in Kitchener, Ontario. *Below:* An informal practice session at Nationals in Kelowna, British Columbia.

"It was stressful," Kate Virtue recalls. "When Tessa was finally allowed to call home she was crying. But she said, 'I'm not crying because I'm sad, I'm crying because I'm so happy to talk to you.'"

Kate, with her own history in ballet, confesses she secretly hoped that her daughter would choose to attend the National Ballet School, but she left that decision to Tessa. And Tessa, reasoning it out herself, turned down the institution that so many other girls her age were dying to attend.

"A big part of me wanted me to do it and if I hadn't been skating with Scott, that's what I would have done," she explains. "I'd already committed to Scott. Our parents didn't ever put

ton. Tessie was that little girl who looked adults right in the eye when she talked to them. She was, and is, open and gregarious but not in a way of grandstanding or showing off. She's imbued with a work ethic, but I don't think she sees it as work. She's excited to get up at 6 a.m. and work for something. She'd watch Jordan's class and afterward she could do, without having tried it, what some of the senior girls at her sister's level were having trouble grasping. So she takes a lot of joy in trying things. Is it hard? Yes it is, but it doesn't scare her. I really think she believes she's dancing when she's skating. It's very soulful. There is an honesty: Tessa believes in every moment she creates, and if she doesn't she

"'This is the first time a nine-year-old has turned down the National Ballet School because she has a partner!'"

— Mavis Staines, Artistic Director, National Ballet School

pressure on us, but if we committed to the season at those yearly meetings we were going to finish the season. And I knew that if I skated, I could still do ballet as a hobby, but that if I went to the National Ballet School there was no way I could continue skating."

"It was a huge decision," Kate recalls. "When she told the school no, that she was committed to her skating partner, Mavis Staines, the artistic director, said, 'This is the first time a nine-year-old has turned down the National Ballet School because she has a partner!'"

The school clearly wanted Tessa to enroll and Mavis Staines telephoned her dance teacher Jennifer Swan in London to find out if there was anything she could do.

"Typically people are chomping at the bit to get into the school," Jennifer recalls. "She really did stand out within our students. But Tessa and her family had already had a lot of reinforcement about skating. The skating world was indicating that they could go places. Tessa is a very loyal person and that commitment she has to her partner and her work is part of her stage presence."

Jennifer continues, "She was cute as a but-

challenges it. She and Scott are both that way with the people they work with."

Tessa auditioned again the following summer, but made the same decision for the same reason, and Kate knew that her daughter would not attend the National Ballet School, although at the yearly spring meetings between the Moirs and Virtues, she kept expecting Tessa to say she wasn't going to maintain the heavy skating commitment because of her other interests. But she never did.

Meanwhile, Scott was demonstrating his faith in the partnership in a different way. Sensitive, emotional, and caring for a boy of his age, Scott took an early liking to ice dancing because of its speed, precision, and intricacy. But he was discovering that he really only liked ice dancing with Tessa Virtue. Paul MacIntosh would have his dance students do "circuits" in which they'd skate a lap with their regular partner, then switch to do a lap with someone else's partner. As he grew older, Scott would also partner other dancers through the various levels of testing. In either situation, his inner reaction was the same. "Every time, I'd say to myself, 'Okay Tessa, come back.' I hated to skate with anyone else but Tess. Those poor girls.

Above: At competition with coaches Suzanne Killing and Paul MacIntosh. *Below:* On the ice before competition in 2000.

I was probably pretty rough on them, because they weren't as good as Tessa and they wouldn't hold themselves as well as Tessa did. And that really frustrated me."

Native ability, Carol Moir's early instruction, and healthy competition between the two youngsters gave Tessa and Scott a solid grounding in core skating skills. They were both fast, had good balance and posture, and were keenly aware of the proper use of edges, so necessary to maintain power and flow and for presenting a unified look below the knees. But when they started working with Paul, "that was when we really built our foundation, that's for sure," Tessa says. "Paul had us doing a ton of stroking and was really breaking it down into the basics of skating."

Paul had taught Suzanne Killing (now Suzanne Killing-Wood) and Peter MacDonald when they were nationally ranked junior ice dancers in the early 1990s. And when Suzanne retired at the age of seventeen, Paul convinced her to pursue her Skate Canada coaching certification. She had been one of the most creative students he'd ever had and had an innate understanding of music and its application to skating. When Tessa and Scott began making their pre-dawn treks from Bethel Church, Suzanne was twenty-three and she and Paul were working together at several different rinks in Kitchener and Waterloo.

"They were eight and ten when they came to Waterloo," recalls Suzanne. Her first impression of Tessa and Scott was that "they were a little vision. There was already talk about them. I knew of Scott, and I was anticipating the third Moir anyway.

"They had a musicality that was different than any other kids I had ever taught. Whether in simple dances or more complex ones, you could see the music was fuller to them more than to the other kids. It wasn't just the (time) count, it was the character and the way they played off each other. Usually at that age you have to get the kids to count out loud to the music — 1-2-3-4 — but I never had to do that with Tessa and Scott. And Tessa, of course, would add her flair."

The young team were still getting most of their ice time in Ilderton and were preparing for the Western Ontario sectionals in the juvenile category, but in late autumn of 1998, just a week before sectionals, Scott broke his right arm playing flag football. (In later years, when Scott was trying to recall the incident, Tessa would

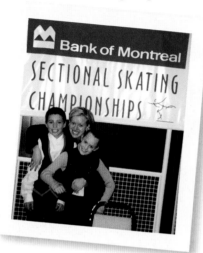

have to remind him which arm he had broken.) "My doctor said to me, 'I'm going to put you in a cast, and you *could* go skating, but this is the arm you have to use for the rest of your life.' My grandfather was with me and he told my parents, 'No way, I was there talking to the doctor, he can't go.' So we had to skip sectionals and decided to go to the all-Ontarios, which is what you do when you can't go to sectionals and then Nationals. We went there and we won that."

"In the scheme of things, it's not that big, but it was big to us at the time," Tessa recalls.

The provincials, held in Woodstock, Ontario, in January 1999, was their first formal victory, and as all competitions would continue to do for the duration of their careers, it whetted their appetite for more.

Scott *didn't* break his arm the following season, and the increased training in Waterloo paid off in a victory at the juvenile sectionals, earning them a berth in Tomorrow's Champions, a prophetic title for the national pre-novice and juvenile championships. The following year, novices would also be added to Tomorrow's Champions, as Skate

Canada tried to get its younger stars more attention rather than having them be overshadowed by the juniors and seniors at the regular Canadian Championships.

Both skaters were excited to make their first major trip, to Kelowna, British Columbia, and to get their Western Ontario team jackets. Tessa confesses that one of her main goals as a six-year-old starting her first group classes in Ilderton had been to become good enough to earn one of the jackets, with "Program Assistant" emblazoned on the

"WE WERE IN IT FOR ALL THE PERKS. WE WANTED TO SEE KELOWNA, WANTED TO WEAR OUR JACKETS, WANTED TO BE PART OF THE TEAM. IT WAS SO EXCITING, THE WHOLE EXPERIENCE. BUT WHEN WE GOT OUT ON THE ICE I WAS SO NERVOUS. —*Scott*

back, that were given to helpers in the CanSkate program. Now she had a more important jacket of her own.

"That was our breakthrough," Scott said of qualifying for Tomorrow's Champions. "We were scared, though. The size thing was a huge factor for us. And we'd never been in a national competition before, so we had no idea how we'd place."

"And it was a big rink with lights and judging stands," Tessa adds.

"We were usually in such c-o-o-o-l-l-l-ld arenas, and Tess would be shaking; a dark, hometown hockey rink," Scott continues. "We were in it for all the perks. We wanted to see Kelowna, wanted to wear our jackets, wanted to be part of the team. It was so exciting, the whole experience. But when we got out on the ice I was so nervous. Scared. I can remember looking up in the stands and Paul was talking to us and I wasn't listening at all. He was saying, '*Hel-lo*, you're at the national championships!'"

In order to foster proper grounding in the sport, juvenile and pre-novice championships are made up of two compulsory dances and a

Top: In Vienna, Austria, before a
formal practice session.
Middle: With Paul at Tomorrow's
Champions competition.
Bottom: Posing for photos after gold medal
win at Tomorrow's Champions competition, 2000.
Opposite: With Suzanne Killing after a win at
Juvenile Sectionals, 1999.

Above: (left to right) Alma, Tessa, Scott, Carol, and Kate after gold medal win.
Right: In Vienna, Austria, March 2000.
Opposite: On the ice during a competition.

"combination" free skate. In that limited free skate, couples must skate a pattern of a prescribed dance — in Kelowna that year it was the Ten-Fox — and then proceed to steps of their own creation. Tessa and Scott weren't expecting to win, nor were they expected by insiders to win. But at the end of the compulsory dances, they stood first.

"We were thinking, 'Oh, wow, we've got a chance to win this,'" Scott says. "But then we went back to our parents to say how cool that is, they said 'Well, yeah, it is cool but it doesn't really matter where you come, it's just about skating well and having fun.' We went out there and said, 'Let's do this thing,' and we ended up winning. We were the youngest team in the championship, and on the podium we were the shortest. I remember standing with my hands stretched in the air so I could put them around the shoulders of the other couples. We were juvenile national champions and even though it didn't really mean that much, I was thinking, 'Oh, wow, I really like this competing thing. I really like competitive ice dancing, and we

can really do something with this. NOW I want to win pre-novice.'"

"I didn't have the same realization as Scott, not at that point," Tessa says. "I had fun in Kelowna and I met a lot of people. But in those early years, the absolute best part of any of it for me was the choreography. It was so much fun and I just lived for that."

The unexpected championship in Kelowna was a watershed moment for the young couple. It was then that those closest to them had their first inkling that something special might be percolating for Tessa and Scott. When the event opened, Kate Virtue, who was new to this level of skating competition, had found herself hoping only that they wouldn't finish dead last. But she was assured by Alma Moir, as she watched group after group, that their children weren't going to be "last or even second last. They're as good as this group." Carol Moir recalls thinking, "Wow, they're either really very good or everyone else is very bad." And she didn't believe it was the latter. Alma Moir knew

"THEY WERE SO LITTLE AND SO YOUNG,
BUT MOSTLY LITTLE, BUT THEY SKATED BIG." —*Alma Moir*

they were good, but as a veteran of skating she also knew that judges can have their own priorities and preconceptions, especially in ice dancing. "They were so little and so young, but mostly little," Alma says. "But they skated big." Suzanne and Paul were surprised at how far their team — and it was now *their* team — had come in such a short time. Paul told "Skate Canada officials and anyone who would listen, 'You're never going to see a rise in a dance team like this one.'"

In their first exposure to the country's best young talent, Tessa and Scott were also studying how to act like a dance team. They watched the pre-novices and imitated them in terms of warming up, how to bow to the audience, even how to get onto the ice from the other side of the boards.

Tessa and Scott continued to train individually in singles with Carol, and she told both of them that had they not succeeded in ice dancing, they would have been excellent free skaters.

Above: Suzanne and Tessa in 1999.

Scott still urges young dancers to continue in singles as long as they can and feels that's even more important with the demanding technically based skill sets required under the code of points judging system, which was implemented in 2004.

In Waterloo, they learned essential fundamentals of body positioning, edge quality, speed, and blade control from Paul. "I was training Danny then, and one thing about the Moirs: they're real boys," Paul says. "They're kind of crazy and out there, but are very willing to participate in things that are not just simple training. I tried to keep Scott under control with his training so later in life he'd be good at it, and it worked. He's a training animal now. I was the technician and Suzanne was the creative force."

While Paul pushed them in the discipline of technique, Suzanne pushed them even harder on the artistic side of ice dancing.

"Suz had us trying crazy things: trying to twiz-zle as fast as possible and doing dips and fun moves and really creative things," recalls Tessa, who revelled in the process. "We were doing things that were probably too advanced for our skill level, but at the same time it was a real challenge. That made us better and it made it really fun. She'd show us something and ask, 'Can you do that?' And we'd think she was crazy because there was no way we were doing footwork and changes that fast. For so long, we couldn't do it but we'd just work away and get better. Doing those things that were advanced and different and creative, I really think that those early programs started us off right."

With Tessa's affinity for choreography and love of dance, she was immediately drawn to Suzanne and, despite their age difference, the feeling was mutual. At a party in Ilderton to celebrate the 1999 novice title won by Sheri and Danny Moir, Suzanne and Tessa spent most of the evening together on the dance floor creating an add-on dance, where one person does four steps, the other adds four more, and so on. "I thought, 'This is the start of a really good friendship,'" Suzanne says.

If Suzanne and Paul split their coaching team roughly along technical and creative lines, their dance team did the same thing. Scott, through practice and DNA, was firmly grounded in "pure skating," while Tessa's background in ballet and modern dance ignited her interest in the choreographic side.

"For sure," she says. "Choreography comes naturally to Scott too, but he's more technical," Tessa says. "I might say to him, 'So, I want to hover around you like a butterfly,' and he could figure out how to make it work. But he's also so musical, and he's not even conscious of it."

In fact, Scott has often been compared to four-time world champion Kurt Browning in that sense: a skater who at the beginning of his career was known mostly for his technical and athletic

"[SCOTT IS] MORE TECHNICAL.
I MIGHT SAY TO HIM, 'SO, I WANT TO HOVER AROUND
YOU LIKE A BUTTERFLY,' AND HE COULD FIGURE OUT
HOW TO MAKE IT WORK." —*Tessa*

Above: Posing on the ice during a photoshoot, 2000.

prowess, but who had a natural feel for music and artistry that began to exhibit itself as he became more mature. Over time, Scott became a larger contributor to the choreographic process and Tessa went through a similar growth process on the technical side, but in their early years in Waterloo they were guided by their natural tendencies. The most dominant of those tendencies was their competitiveness, both as a team and as individuals. That was an important asset because it kept both of them striving to become better, eliminating one of the major causes of dance and pairs teams splitting up: an inequality of ability. Almost no championship couple, outside of brother–sister teams,

They became the fastest, a process that had started a few years earlier. Paul and Suzanne had a "tween" couple on their hands who were fast, naturally talented, born performers, competitive with themselves and with each other, driven to win, and respectful of their coaches' abilities.

"They always understood, and took what you were saying and applied it," Suzanne says. "There was an acceptance of what you said, and they just did it. Normally kids have excuses; that it's too hard, their partner isn't ready, they don't have the confidence. But their friendship together, to really know that your partner is there for you, instills a confidence that most partnerships don't

"WE WERE ALWAYS THE SMALLEST AND WE ALWAYS MADE A POINT OF PROVING THAT WE WEREN'T THE SLOWEST." —*Scott*

start as young and last as long as Tessa and Scott have. Often, the best duos are assembled after it has become clear they will be of roughly equal calibre.

"There was a time when Scott was light years ahead of me," Tessa says. "And there was also a time when everyone was worried that I was going to outgrow Scott. In those early years I always felt like I was playing catch-up. Until our early teens, I would say."

"I felt exactly the same way," Scott says, with some amazement. "I felt like I was always a step behind you. And I had to step it up. I remember that feeling, but I never remember you having to catch up at all. We were very blessed in both of those areas: we pretty much grew together."

"Another part of it was that, until very recently, we were always the smallest team," Tessa adds. "The tiniest. Immature and young. Maybe that pushed us because we always felt we had something to prove."

"We were always the smallest," adds Scott, "and we always made a point of proving that we weren't the slowest."

have. They had problems like any other partnership, but they knew they were committed and they had a willingness to believe. That trust grows over the years, but I think you have to come built that way in the first place."

The fact that they were winning competitions helped reinforce the trust in each other and in their coaches. As soon as they were juvenile champions, they set their sights on the pre-novice title, even though the age gap between them and most of the other teams would be even wider than it had been in juvenile. In 2001, Tomorrow's Champions was held at the Kitchener Auditorium, an older, intimate arena known as "The Aud." Tessa and Scott weren't expected to win; traditionally ice dancers rarely triumphed in their first year at any level, even if they were the best on that particular evening. But Tessa and Scott defied the odds — and history — and won the pre-novice championship over a field of older opponents. In the process, they gave their first of what would eventually become hundreds of TV interviews. Immediately, they reset their sights

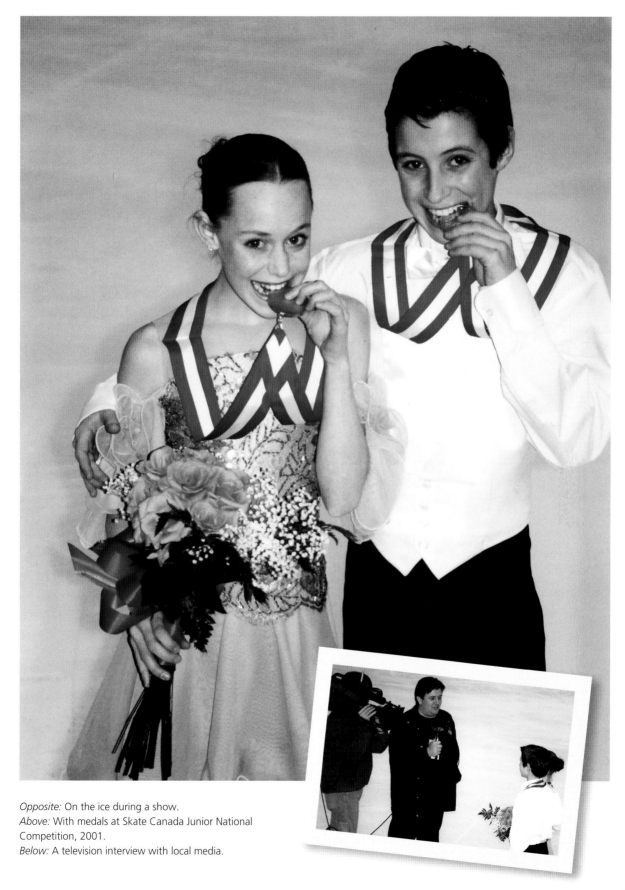

Opposite: On the ice during a show.
Above: With medals at Skate Canada Junior National Competition, 2001.
Below: A television interview with local media.

Above: Tessa and Scott wearing "Canada" athletic clothing. *Opposite:* On the ice during the National Championships, 2002.

another three years at junior before finally reaching senior skating. "And that's the good ones," Carol Moir says. That delayed process was expected to be even more pronounced for a couple who would be only twelve and fourteen when the 2002 novice championships in Newfoundland rolled around.

"We used that protocol thing in their training," Suzanne remembers. "For motivation and planning and to stretch them we would say: 'We'll go out and do everything we can and *dare* them not to put us first.' It's not that they expected to finish first, but we wanted to get people wondering why they didn't."

At the same time, Suzanne was working diligently at getting Tessa and Scott to fully understand each other and what they had together. She would hold regular meetings where each partner could clear the air, or grapple out loud with something that had been bothering them. Those meetings continued until they were well beyond their mid-teens, proving to be invaluable both then and later on in their careers.

"I'd try to make them understand that any relationship, marriage, business partnership, skating partnership, whatever, is a challenge," Suzanne explains. "When you get young people working toward a common goal that's very important. I tried to get them to appreciate each other as individuals, to know that they needed each other and that it didn't matter if one had excelled at something and the other didn't. They were in it together."

Tessa and Scott already had the natural tendency to treat each other with respect and affection, but as Tessa recalls, "We were young teenagers, a boy and a girl trying to work together as a team. So that's when we started figuring out what the other brings to the relationship and, well, not fighting, but we were banging up against each other."

"We were starting to be opinionated," Scott says. "I remember when I was a young boy and I'd see the older guys fighting with their partners. It took a couple of years to figure out that was not the way it should be. We never really fought on the ice, but Suzanne was a big part of getting through that stage and making us realize that we're both in it for the same reasons, that we need to work

to focus on the novice ranks they would move into for the 2001–2 season. They remained focused on the task at hand and never thought of how they were rocketing toward the upper echelons of Canadian skating, or of what was happening on the international scene they might be joining one day.

"We saw what we were chasing," Scott shrugs. "We didn't really see past that at all, which is probably a good thing. I don't think we ever compared ourselves to the world champions of the time. But every competition we were in, I'd go out there and say to myself, 'How can I compete against these guys?' And then we would compete and beat them."

They were about to enter novice skating, which in ice dancing meant a dramatic change in approach. For the first time they would be required — or, from their viewpoint, finally be allowed — to perform a regular free skate in competition. As well, ice dancing's hierarchy and "protocol judging" (keeping skaters in the spot they're expected to finish) tend to kick in at the novice level. Most couples were expected to spend at least two years in novice before they'd get to the podium, and move up to

together on the ice, and that it's important to get along. And that's something we carried with us all the way through."

"On the ice we're together," Tessa adds, "but off the ice we continued to grow in different directions, so Suz sat us down once or twice a week and we'd review things: She'd ask, 'Tell me how this made you feel when he said this,' or, 'Scott, how did you feel when she did this?' Suz can really take credit for helping us get our business relationship and our working relationship straight. We had to learn that distinction at a very young age, and she gave us the opportunity to talk about things and feel open. It's a part of our relation-

ship people don't see. It is like a marriage in the sense that it takes a lot of work, and that was a big part of who we became. And no one knows that. Everyone knows that we're best friends now, but with all those transitions that you're going through individually and as you're trying to make it work on the ice, there were times we didn't get along. We're such different people in the way we handle things. It's taken almost until now to know exactly how we each deal with things and how to respond accordingly. I learned then that because Scott is so passionate and so intense — I mean, he's a goofy guy and fun-loving, but on the ice he's so intense and takes things so seriously — that sometimes if things aren't working he just needs to blow off steam. Whether that means skating away or yelling or kicking the ice or whatever. Scott wears his feelings on his sleeve."

Tessa admits that at certain points in their pre- and early teen years they were both scared that the partnership might not succeed.

"We had a rough patch," she said. "Now we know that when you're together for so long, there are some ups and downs. But at the time you think, 'Can we work together? Is this going to happen?'"

"Tessa is able to put her emotions aside and think practically," Scott says. Tessa will say, "'Okay, it didn't go well but let's fix it so next time it will

go well.' Over the years I've tried to pick that up because it makes more sense. My natural reaction would be to just go nuts. Go wild, shut down, and get mad."

In Waterloo, they began to recognize that while what they shared — natural chemistry, steadfast friendship, competitive drive, devotion to improving every day — was their greatest strength, how they differed also helped produce a more complete partnership. Essentially, Tessa says, he brings the passion and energy, and she has a calming effect. And such contrasts are usually at the root of all great art.

Even though Tessa and Scott were just twelve and fourteen, Suzanne knew that she had to design a mature free skating program for them as they prepared for their first novice season.

"We were competing with people who are portraying adults," Tessa explains.

Suzanne chose the Cancan, loaded it with fast footwork, and combined two difficult pieces of music, the first of which was a tango. "People doubted the choice of the tango," she recalls. "It's a mature dance, and they were really young and two feet high."

Tessa loved it. Always advanced choreographically, she embraced the "adultness" of the program. They were young, and looked it, and were still worried about her growing too tall, but they had taken a big step forward. They weren't projecting "cute" any more, they were projecting intimacy.

"The tango was the first program in which we had our foreheads together, and we were getting closer to moves that older skaters were doing," she says. "And it had the fastest footwork we'd ever tried to do, or even seen. Although we didn't know it at the time, I think that made a difference in the larger scheme of things because the tango has such a quick tempo, but you also have to be intimate. We really started to get the flavour of it."

Left: A break during practice.
Above: (left to right) Charlie, Tessa, Jordan, and Scott.
Right: Scott at the top of the podium.

Opposite: Travelling in Vienna.
Above: With Suzanne at novice invitational in Vienna, Austria, 2000.
Below: On the ice, during competition in Vienna.

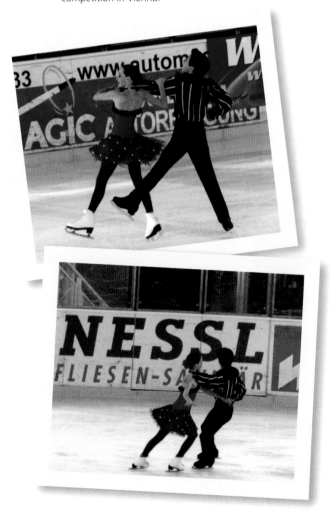

And the tango called for a lot of on-ice acting beyond their years. They were portraying fully developed characters. Many fourteen-year-old boys would not have been able to find the abandon to allow themselves to become the character Scott had to play.

"Suzanne was great with me," Scott recalls. "She would tell me what she thought the part should be and she would give me an avenue, so that I could express what she wanted, but in my own way. I had a lot of help. Trying to keep up with Tessa's expressiveness was tough."

But he managed it. They travelled to Newfoundland for Tomorrow's Champions with the Canadian skating community anticipating that they would make an impression — staking out future ground, but certainly not reaching the podium. Once again, they outstripped expectations and finished a close third. "They fell," Paul MacIntosh says, "or they could have finished first."

Scott was angry about not winning the title and wanted to return to novice the next season to capture gold. But Paul and Suzanne had already decided they should fast-track the team to junior. "Don't hold these kids back," Suzanne advised. Alma Moir, though, was against the jump, worrying that they were "so little" for junior skating. But as she had said before, they were skating big.

Shortly after Tomorrow's Champions, the Western Ontario Section sent Tessa and Scott to a novice invitational in Vienna, their first overseas event. It wasn't an official International Skating Union (ISU) event, but many European dance officials were in attendance. Scott calls it the worst competition of their lives because they hadn't really trained for it: "We skated the first forty seconds well and then ten seconds into the Cancan, it fell apart. We were winning after compulsories in the first European competition of our lives. We had a slip-up in the free dance and then just chased each other around the ice for the next minute. It was *embarrassing*. First in compulsories, fourth overall."

The winners were talented Americans Meryl Davis, two years older than Tessa, and Charlie White, six weeks younger than Scott. They didn't foresee it then, but the two couples would go head-to-head

"'THERE'S NO REASON — AS LONG AS TESSA DOESN'T GROW TOO MUCH — THAT THESE TWO CAN'T BE AT THE OLYMPICS IN 2010.'"—*Suzanne Killing*

several more times over the next eight years, on the biggest skating stages the world has to offer.

While the skaters were disappointed in their performance in Vienna, their coaches were not. They felt the program created a buzz and "captured so many eyes."

The 2001–2 season — an Olympic year that produced the pairs judging scandal in Salt Lake City that was linked to vote-buying in the ice dance event — was drawing to a close. Tessa and Scott had now arrived at a crossroads, and had a difficult decision to make. They were about to enter junior competition, in which the best skaters were training full time, five days a week, several hours a day. Tessa and Scott couldn't afford that kind of time, and couldn't spend so many hours commuting. She was about to enter her final year of elementary

school, and he'd just had the "best year" of his school life as a freshman at Medway High School in nearby Arva, but they knew they couldn't properly pursue their goals if they kept on as they were. So, at the annual Virtue–Moir meeting, the families agreed: Tessa and Scott had to move to Waterloo.

Something else was brought up for the first time that spring, something that might have been brewing in the minds of Tessa and Scott but hadn't been mentioned aloud.

"Jim Virtue wanted to see the ultimate plan," Suzanne says, recalling that everyone knew Vancouver was bidding to host the 2010 Winter Games, but that the site had not yet been chosen.

"And I said to him, 'There's no reason — as long as Tessa doesn't grow too much — that these two can't be at the Olympics in 2010.'"

"IT WAS LIKE WE WERE ON THIS LITTLE ADVENTURE. YOU'RE WITH A TEAM, YOU GET THE CANADA JACKETS, AND YOU'RE TRAVELLING: YOU'RE THIRTEEN YEARS OLD AND YOU'RE GOING TO SEE SLOVAKIA, CROATIA, AND HOLLAND." —*Tessa*

Chapter Three

THE CLASS OF THE ICE

THE YOUNG COUPLE FACED DIFFICULT CHALLENGES, BUT THEY WERE SUSTAINED BY THEIR LOVE FOR SKATING AND THE KNOWLEDGE THAT THEY COULD BE CHAMPIONS.

TESSA LIKES THE AGE-OLD DESCRIPTION OF A duck: calm on the surface, but paddling like the dickens underneath. It speaks to the art of making tortuous ice dancing manoeuvres look easy and pleasurable, and it also describes how, on the way to medals and championships, skaters must make great sacrifices and overcome serious obstacles that the public knows nothing about.

Moving away from home is never easy, at any age, but when you're entering the teen years, the most social part of your life, it's particularly difficult to leave family and friends to move to another city. But Tessa and Scott had to face that painful separation in September 2002 when they left London and Ilderton to enroll at Bluevale Collegiate Institute in Waterloo, Ontario.

They were both billeting in excellent family situations: Scott with Bev and Grace Strachan, and Tessa joining fellow ice dancer Bronwyn Williams at the home of Kitchener-Waterloo skating club coach Becky Babb and her husband Scott Strachan. That eased the worry for the Moir and Virtue families, and so did the knowledge that, as Alma Moir describes it, "Tessa and Scott could look out for each other."

Still, there were a lot of adjustments for thirteen- and fifteen-year-olds.

Left: Tessa and Scott posing for a photo before travelling to a competition. *Opposite:* Tessa and Scott attending a banquet dinner held during a competition in Andorra, 2005.

"It was a big time of our lives and we were both scared," Scott concedes. "We were together a lot during that time. Not only were we skating partners, but we were really each other's family because we were more or less alone in Kitchener-Waterloo."

Tessa should have still been in elementary school, but she was a good student and received permission from London's Stoneybrook Public School to skip grade eight and enter high school a year early. (She did return to London at the end of the year to watch from the audience as the kids she'd known since kindergarten graduated from

Above: With coach Paul MacIntosh.
Opposite: Tessa and Scott enjoy some free time outdoors.

grade eight. It was difficult for her, her mother recalls, but education and friends are important to Tessa and she wanted to be there for their big day.)

"We were already comfortable in the rink setting in Waterloo because we had been commuting," Tessa recalls. "School was the biggest thing. There were so many skaters who would go from the rink right to the high school. It sounds funny now, but that was basically why I skipped grade eight, so I could get rides with them, and so I could have first-period spare and skate in the morning.

"I remember the first day of grade nine very well: I was missing two teeth, I was walking up these big steps to what seemed like a huge school, I didn't know anyone, didn't know where I was going, didn't know what classes I was taking and I

was feeling like I was missing out because I didn't get the grade eight experience. I remember sitting by myself at lunch before I made any friends. And Scott and I were going home on weekends, so we weren't around to socialize then. I think girls are different that way. If you miss one minute of the weekend time then you're out of the loop and I felt out of the loop going in. Grade nine was tough, but grade ten was my favourite year. By then it was home to me and I was comfortable and made so many friends. And I actually went back to that prom when they all graduated, even though I only went there for grade nine and ten."

Scott had spent grade nine at Medway High School in Arva, Ontario, about eight kilometres from Bethel Church, where he and Tessa had passed four years waiting for each other to go to pre-dawn practices.

"Ninth grade was the best year I can remember. At the end of that year I was sad, because I knew I wanted to get better at skating and I wanted to push to the next level of junior, but that meant I would have to leave. That was tough, but it was worth it. When you're a kid, high school's the thing, and if you're not there you think you're missing out on so much. At Bluevale I had one friend who was also a skater (Andrew Poje), so I hung out with him. I met almost no one in tenth grade because I didn't want to make new friends, because I already had my friends at home. They were all city kids in Waterloo, and I missed my country buddies."

Tessa and Scott never had the same lunch periods, so he was unable to help her with that first-year lunchtime loneliness, but otherwise they spent more time than ever together, further solidifying an already sturdy friendship. Their lockers were right next to each other. Tessa would encourage Scott with his schoolwork, "and when I'd get down she'd help me. And sometimes the other way around."

A month before school started, Tessa and Scott took care of some unfinished business by winning the Lake Placid International novice dance competition. The previous summer, they had competed in their first international at Lake Placid,

"IT WAS A BIG TIME OF OUR LIVES AND WE WERE BOTH SCARED. WE WERE TOGETHER A LOT DURING THAT TIME. NOT ONLY WERE WE SKATING PARTNERS, BUT WE WERE REALLY EACH OTHER'S FAMILY BECAUSE WE WERE MORE OR LESS ALONE IN KITCHENER-WATERLOO." —*Scott*

Above: Performing compulsory dance program.
Opposite: During competition at the Lake Placid International dance competition, 2002.

the famous Adirondack site of two Winter Olympics. They'd finished third, but the two memories that linger for them are the excitement of hearing "Canada" after their names for the first time when they were introduced to skate and getting the little Canadian flag stickers attached to their skate boots.

They had been launched into the junior ranks because Paul and Suzanne wanted to keep challenging them and junior offered what novice didn't: the Original Dance (OD) program. It's the middle of the three ice dance segments, and corresponds to the short program in singles and pairs. The technical elements are dictated by the rules, and each year the ISU ice dance technical committee selects a rhythm that all couples must use, but the program design is left to the individual couples.

Suzanne designed a waltz OD, skated to Bach's "Les Poissons" from the Disney movie *The Little Mermaid* for their first year in junior. Paul still considers it among her best pieces of work. Tessa loved it, "because of the dress mostly," she laughs. "I like fashion, for sure, but when it comes down to it I like elegant things, classical things. And that carries over onto the ice. Scott likes to wear something pretty simple when he's skating."

"I'm just a basic guy, I guess," Scott quips. "She always looks wonderful so there's no need for me to."

That relatively simple elegance quickly became their trademark costume style — Suzanne made some of Tessa's costumes in those years — but there's far more to it than just personal preference. Since the early 1990s ice dancing, particularly in the international arena, had begun to resemble a high-end Halloween party, with costuming often overshadowing the athletic components of the performance.

"We had this understanding with Suzanne and with Paul that we wanted to let our skating speak for itself on the ice," Tessa confirms. "It's who we are as people as well."

The young Canadians could let their skating speak for itself because it had a strong and pure voice. It focused on the lower body;

Left: In Croatia, 2003.

the superb control of their blade edges; precise, quick transitions; knees as soft as cotton batten; and ever-increasing speed.

Paul knew that "Tessa and Scott would suffer for a year," with the jump to junior skating, and he was right. Smaller and younger than the rest of the competitors in the field, they finished seventh at Nationals in Saskatoon.

"The step up to junior was huge," Scott recalls. "This was the big Nationals."

Although they finished seventh, it was a very positive experience. Tessa fondly recalls sitting in the area where skaters wait for their marks to appear on the scoreboard (commonly known as the "kiss and cry") at a senior nationals for the first time, excitedly repeating, "That was so much fun, that was so much fun," after the Original Dance. "We loved to skate in front of people," she says, which would have come as no surprise to Alma Moir, who recalls that even when they were very young "the more crowded the arena was and the noisier it was, the more they both liked it. I once told Scott if skating didn't work out maybe he could be an actor."

Tessa remembers sitting by the boards when the senior dancers were doing their Golden Waltzes. "It was so fast. There was wind every time they skated by. That was the first time we'd watched a senior event live. They were so big, so fast."

And so accessible.

"We were riding the elevator with Marie-France and Patrice, and I nudged Tess and said, 'Hey, check it out.'"

"And Shae-Lynn and Victor," Tessa adds.

Canadian ice dancers Marie-France Dubreuil and Patrice Lauzon won five national titles and were silver medallists at the 2006 and 2007 world championships before retiring and getting married. Shae-Lynn Bourne and Victor Kraatz would go from their tenth national title in Saskatoon to winning the world championships in Washington less than two months later. Their victory over reigning champions Irina Lobacheva and Ilia Averbukh was a major turning point in ice dancing history. It was the first time since ice dancing had become an official world

championship discipline in 1952 that a couple from anywhere other than Europe had taken gold. And since 1970, Russian couples had dominated the discipline. Although five other non-Russians did win titles in the next thirty-three years, only Jayne Torvill and Christopher Dean, widely considered to be the greatest ice dancers of all time, made a significant dent in Russian domination of the event. Bourne and Kraatz's silver medal in 2002 was the highest finish by any team from North America in thirty-two years, although many skating insiders felt that Canada's Tracy Wilson and Rob McCall deserved at least one world championship (1988),

concentrating only on the junior teams directly in front of them.

One of those teams was Siobhan Karam and Joshua McGrath, who were junior bronze medallists in 2003 and would enter the following season as the favourites. They trained in Michigan under Russian expatriates Igor Shpilband, a former world junior ice dance champion, and Marina Zoueva, who had spent many years living and coaching in Ottawa. With Tessa and Scott planning a Russian medley free dance for the 2003–4 season, Paul asked Marina if she would spend some time with his couple to work on the authenticity of their

> "WE HAD THIS UNDERSTANDING WITH SUZANNE AND WITH PAUL THAT WE WANTED TO LET OUR SKATING SPEAK FOR ITSELF ON THE ICE. IT'S WHO WE ARE AS PEOPLE AS WELL." —*Tessa*

and that Bourne and Kraatz could have had one or two before they created history in Washington. But ice dancing, with far fewer falls than the other disciplines, was prey to more subjective judging, which in turn could often lead to "protocol judging" and, at worst, deal-making.

But none of that mattered to Tessa and Scott; it wasn't even on their radar. As they grew into their ice dancing careers, Canada had three world-class teams — Shae-Lynn Bourne and Victor Kraatz; Marie-France Dubreuil and Patrice Lauzon; and Megan Wing and Aaron Lowe — and an American couple, Ben Agosto skating with transplanted Canadian Tanith Belbin, were making a meteoric rise up the junior ranks. "Until after our own Olympics we never really put it together that none of them had ever won an Olympics," Scott said. Furthermore, Tessa and Scott were deliberately

dance. "I took them to Marina and she kind of played with them for a day, and she was brilliant with them," Paul recalls. "I knew they'd be direct competition to Siobhan and Josh the next junior Nationals, even if Marina and Igor didn't."

Officials at Skate Canada must have sensed something too. After finishing only seventh in their junior debut, Tessa and Scott were hoping to receive a junior Grand Prix assignment for the 2003 fall season. But they were scheduled for two Grand Prix events: Skate Slovakia in Bratislava in mid-September, and the Croatia Cup in Zagreb a month later. There was also the possibility of junior Worlds in The Hague in early March. Before any of those events, though, they were assigned to the North American Challenge Cup in the late summer in Thornhill, Ontario, a suburb bordering Toronto's northern limits. They won handily, as

Opposite: Hugging on the ice at Nationals, 2004. *Above:* With Paul during the 2003–4 season.

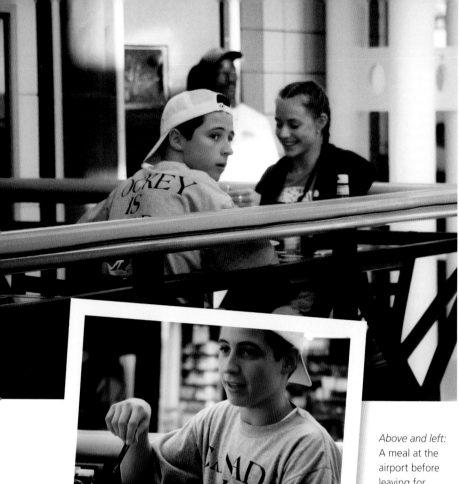

Above and left:
A meal at the
airport before
leaving for
competition.

they were impressed with the way their children skated in their first major international, they also "saw how young they were compared to everyone else," Alma explains. For instance, both the gold and silver medallist teams were made up of men and women who would be nineteen before the calendar year was out. The parents were concerned about their barely teenaged kids, "so Kate and I made a pact that there'd always be one parent who would go to the events."

Moreover, Bratislava just happened to be where the ISU dance committee was staging a weekend seminar to help judges prepare for the radical new "International Judging System," which had been fast-tracked after the judging scandal at the 2002 Olympic Games.

For more than a century, skating had used the heavily subjective 6.0 marking system through which judges were able to defend questionable rankings to referees with little more than "I liked them better." ISU president Ottavio Cinquanta demanded a more objective system, and put pressure on his staff to accelerate the process after the embarrassment of the judging scandal in Salt Lake City. The new and fundamentally different system, most of it designed and perfected in Canada, was to come into use for the 2004 Worlds and Grand Prix events. Canada would introduce it for the 2005 Nationals. It is a complex, computer-based concept, but the founding principle is that almost every element or movement of a program is marked against an established standard, not against other skaters. There are certain "levels" of skills, identified by "callers" who sit near the judging panel. Skaters start their program at zero and have points added for what they've done

Canadian dancers took four of the top five spots in the cross-border junior competition.

"It was like we were on this little adventure," Tessa said. "You're with a team, you get the Canada jackets, and you're travelling: you're thirteen years old and you're going to see Slovakia, Croatia, and Holland."

Scott points out that once skaters reach senior they don't get to visit many of the countries they'd see on the Junior Grand Prix circuit, because they're not part of skating's Big Six — Russia, China, Japan, Canada, the United States, and France — which play host to the senior Grand Prix events.

At the first Junior Grand Prix event of their careers in Slovakia, Tessa and Scott finished sixth. But the ultimate importance of Skate Slovakia to Tessa and Scott's career could not be measured by placement. For one thing, both Alma Moir and Kate Virtue had travelled to Bratislava, and while

Above: With Paul MacIntosh in Bratislava, Slovakia, 2003. *Bottom right:* Alma Moir and Kate Virtue in Slovakia.
Bottom left: Team Canada *(back row, left to right):* Carol Hopper, John Mattatall, Christopher Maybee, Cedric Demers, Scott; *(front row):* Dr. Susan Blatz, Megan Duhamel, Ashton Tessier, Tessa, and Terra Findlay.

rather than starting at 6.0 and having points subtracted on some undefined basis. A computer randomly selects which judges' scores will count in the official tally. And individual judges are never identified by their marks, which might increase public suspicion, but protects the judges from the deal-making, and anger, of their own skating federations. (There have been many instances of a federation asking its own judges to go against their consciences and give a higher or lower mark to particular skaters, just to accommodate a deal.)

The new system was made to be far more objective, it was made to reward performance rather than reputation, and it was made to encourage faster, more all-round skating skills.

In short, it was tailor-made for Tessa Virtue and Scott Moir, who were fast, energetic, and well-grounded in every aspect of ice dancing, and clearly upwardly mobile.

Their Original Dance during the 2003 season was a combination of the classic 1950s rock tunes "Tears on My Pillow" and "Tutti Frutti" and contained the usual speed and difficult footwork.

"Two delegates from the ISU committee, from Italy and Ukraine, stormed through people to find me," Paul MacIntosh recalls, "just to say that Tessa and Scott's OD was exactly the way the committee had envisioned things for the new system."

Whatever the scoring system, it can never hurt skaters to have judges believing that they're the ones who are capable of satisfying it.

T HE NEXT MONTH, TESSA AND SCOTT WERE fourth at the Croatia Cup. They returned to Kitchener for more intense training, then headed to Edmonton in January for the Nationals. They were no longer in awe of the competition and won the title. Looking back, Tessa and Scott recognize that was a pivotal moment in their careers. Winning the Nationals sent them to international events as champions of a major skating nation, and gave

them enormous confidence, and established them as a team on a meteoric rise. They were named to the team for junior Worlds at The Hague in early March, but first they travelled to Halifax to spend a few days with Suzanne, who had left Waterloo to begin studies in psychology at Dalhousie University. She fine-tuned their programs and it was off to their first Junior Worlds, where they finished a respectable eleventh. Scott felt they skated reasonably well and was most encouraged by their solid free dance, which would provide them a tailwind heading into the next season, when they would begin yet another climb: this time up the senior ranks.

Above: Spending time with Suzanne in Halifax, 2004.

"That was probably my favourite competition," Tessa recalls. "My entire family was there, and we went to Amsterdam afterward. It seemed like more than a competition."

For Paul it was finally time to take a breather and reflect upon how far his young team had come in less than a year: "We had been working at this a long time, but it was a real whirlwind of seven months when they took skating by storm. They were eleventh at Junior Worlds, but you knew they were better than eleventh and they would certainly surpass the other competitors."

Those were prophetic words, but by the time they came true Tessa and Scott would no longer be skating in Waterloo or with Paul as their coach.

That spring, after six years of working in Waterloo and two years of living there full-time, Tessa and Scott decided they needed to change training venues. Suzanne had already moved to Halifax, removing a piece of the coaching equation that had worked so well. And even Paul concedes that while he was doing well with other teams without Suzanne, "I probably couldn't have done it with those two."

"At that time we were basically the top team in Waterloo," Tessa explains. "There weren't the big star teams ahead of us that were motivating us. We grew up with that, and it makes a big difference in the training atmosphere. We needed to go somewhere where there were teams that were better than us."

1990. Marina had worked as a choreographer with the incomparable pairs skaters Ekaterina Gordeeva and Sergei Grinkov, the legendary husband and wife duo who won two Olympic championships. She was on the ice in Moscow the day they first skated together in 1981, and was the only other person on the Lake Placid practice ice with "G & G" in November 1995 when Sergei collapsed and died.

"Even the first time Tessa and Scott came to Michigan just to try us as coaches, I felt their spirit, the same spirit, the same image as Katia and Sergei," Zoueva once told the *Hamilton Spectator* "Man and woman on ice. The chemistry. Man and woman in sync. It has never happened in ice dance before like this. Our sport with the new judging system is 50 percent sport, 50 percent art, and this pair represents that harmony."

"THERE WEREN'T THE BIG STAR TEAMS AHEAD OF US THAT WERE MOTIVATING US. WE GREW UP WITH THAT, AND IT MAKES A BIG DIFFERENCE IN THE TRAINING ATMOSPHERE. WE NEEDED TO GO SOMEWHERE WHERE THERE WERE TEAMS THAT WERE BETTER THAN US." —*Tessa*

They were prepared to test drive a number of different coaching situations and decided to start with Canton, Michigan, because they had already worked with Marina Zoueva and because it was only two and a half hours from their western Ontario homes. They went to Michigan for a couple of days, felt they could work with Marina and her coaching partner Igor Shpilband, and agreed to return for another two-week stretch after school was over for the summer. Tessa sensed that Marina and Igor were also testing them out a bit too, gauging them as potential students.

"We liked it, so we didn't have to try anywhere else," Scott says. "They were good about it. We had just beaten their team, Siobhan and Josh, but Marina and Igor said, 'We'd love to have you.'"

Igor had won the 1983 world junior ice dance championship with Tatiana Gladkova, skating for the old Soviet Union, but he defected to the U.S. in

Many top North American couples were already training with Marina and Igor, including Canadian silver medallists Megan Wing and Aaron Lowe and American champions Tanith Belbin and Ben Agosto, who would eventually win an Olympic silver medal and four medals at Worlds.

Moving to Waterloo at the ages of thirteen and fifteen, then travelling to Europe to compete, made it slightly easier for Tessa and Scott to move again at fifteen and seventeen, but it was still a major adjustment. If they were looking for a big change, they certainly found it. The skating style Marina and Igor taught was different than they were used to and took some adjustments on Tessa and Scott's part. And Tessa, who is always concerned for the feelings of others, would have felt a certain disloyalty to Suzanne and Paul if she had quickly embraced the new training environment.

"I just needed to get to know people and get comfortable. It took a couple of months."

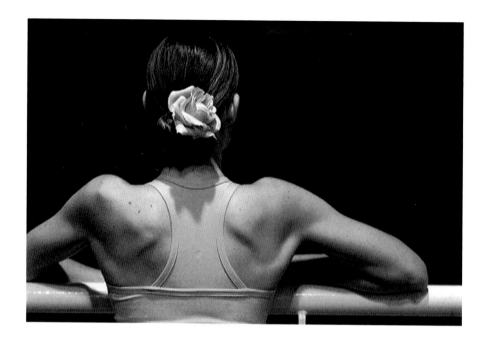

"I JUST NEEDED TO GET TO KNOW PEOPLE AND GET COMFORTABLE. IT TOOK A COUPLE OF MONTHS." —*Tessa*

After so long with Paul and Suzanne, Tessa and Scott had become accustomed to a warm personal relationship with their coaches. The Michigan school was more formal, with more of a barrier between coach and student. Although their relationship with Marina and Igor has since evolved to the point that it's almost a four-person coaching team, the young Canadians, already somewhat intimidated by the setting, were taken aback by the directness, and occasional yelling, of their new coaches.

"They were a lot more aggressive," Scott says. "They don't do subtle. They don't mince words; they don't beat around the bush."

"It took a lot of getting used to," Tessa continues, "especially for me. I want to please. I want them to be happy and I want to do the right thing. And when you don't get that feedback — I think that's what I struggled with at the beginning. It was more rigid, the roles are clear. That's actually great and we really appreciate it now."

Scott moved in with one of the coaches, Brandon Forsyth, and Tessa roomed with pairs skater Tiffany Stiegler, who was five years older. Until Kate Virtue joined her daughter in Canton eight months later, Scott, who had a car, would drive Tessa to the rink, grocery store, and home to western Ontario for the weekends. The three hours they'd spend in the car together, talking about everything but skating, further deepened an already deep relationship.

As they slowly grew more comfortable in their new surroundings, Tessa and Scott were sustained by their love for skating and the knowledge that this was the training ground where they could become national, and perhaps world and Olympic champions. They were stimulated by the contagious energy that bristled through the busy arena from six in the morning until six at night.

They would be competing as seniors at the 2005 Canadian championships (in, of all places, London, Ontario), but they would spend that Grand Prix season, and the one after it, on the junior circuit. That meant balancing training to embrace both competition levels. The junior free skate, for instance, is a three-minute event, while seniors free

Above: Tessa and Scott enjoying free time. *Below:* Sightseeing in Courcheval, France, 2004.
Opposite: Tessa during a training session, 2004.

Above: Celebrating their silver medal win at the Junior Grand Prix competition in Courcheval.

skate for four minutes. The new scoring system, which would eventually be called the Code of Points, was introduced to Grand Prix skating that fall and Nationals in January.

"We liked it right away," Scott says of the new scoring system. "We liked the feedback, how people were getting rewarded for what they were doing. And how clear the levels were. They still had some kinks to work out, but I liked how you could move so much. If you were fourth in compulsories, you could still move up and be first overall. And it was easy for us to see where we could improve. That's one of the best things about the new system. You know exactly where you need to change things and where you can get more points.

"Ever since that season we looked at the marks sheet and said, 'Okay, we're only eleventh right here. Why? Let's fix that and get 'em higher.'"

So Tessa and Scott embraced the Code of Points from its inception, and so did their coaches,

who always stayed on top of the requirements and the annual changes the ISU would make to them. So from the start of the new system, the entire team was ahead of the game rather than trying to catch up to it.

Igor's main focus in the couple's first year with him was to continue to increase their speed and power. "When they came to us, they were still a junior team and they weren't the biggest team or the fastest team and I told them 'you need to become the fastest,' because I thought that was what they needed most," recalls Igor. "I worked with them on basic skating technique. When you have good control and feel secure on your feet, you feel you can go faster.

"They impressed me right away with their ability to relate to each other, their ability to dance, and the difficult things they could do on the ice. And they were very fluid. One of the things they were lacking was the power."

Above: Tessa and Scott after their Grand Prix victory in China, 2004.

Working hard on their speed and their power, Tessa and Scott were soon on their way to becoming the fastest dance team in the world.

In those first few months Igor was learning as much about his new students as they were about him. "First of all, they're very bright kids," he says. "They know exactly what they want and what they need. They're very aware at the rink. They know what everyone is doing around them, they're so tuned in with what goes on with every single person on the ice. That sharpness and awareness really helps them. They're very comfortable on the ice, they're secure on the ice and secure with each other.

"When they first arrived I asked what they should skate their free dance to and they wanted a tango. When they played the piece ("Adios Nonino") for me, I felt it was one you have to be very mature for. There are a lot of very sophisticated tango couples who wouldn't use it, it's so difficult. But they said, 'we want to do it.' So that was

the first free dance I choreographed for them. I thought they were too young to show sophisticated emotion. You don't often find that understanding of music and dance from kids that age."

But with increasing speed and power, they mastered the difficult tango and headed out on the junior Grand Prix circuit.

Their first event was in Courcheval, France, in late August 2004. Tessa and Scott finished second to eventual world junior champions Morgan Matthews and Maxim Zavozin, but beat them in the free dance, a major indicator of their rising status and skill level because the free dance is worth as much in the scoring system as the compulsory and original dance combined.

Paul MacIntosh was also at Courcheval with Alice Graham and Andrew Poje. In practices, Tessa and Scott found it disconcerting to skate past his spot at the boards, where in the past they would have stopped for coaching directions.

"IT WAS THE LOUDEST I'D EVER HEARD AT A COMPETITION. AND THIS WAS THE FIRST TIME THERE WERE SIGNS FOR US." —*Tessa*

While there had been some initial bitterness over their departure from Waterloo, Tessa and Scott were renewing their friendship with Paul. When they headed for their next Grand Prix in northern China — the first real competition of their career that he wouldn't be present for — Paul e-mailed his former students with a reminder of something he used to say to them years earlier: "Be the class of the ice." They won their China event, their first Grand Prix victory, and since then Paul has sent them a similar message before every competition. It is part motivation and part good luck charm, joining Scott's short list of superstitions — new socks for every event — and Tessa's long one: putting the left skate on first; setting her water bottle in the same place on the boards, with her skate guards at the same angle every time; taking the same route through a competition arena every day; keeping a safety pin, always head-up, stuck somewhere in her skating costume.

The first two junior Grand Prix medals of their career qualified them for December's Junior Grand Prix Final in Helsinki, Finland, where they finished second to Matthews and Zavozin, but once again beat them in the free dance. Then, after competing on three different continents that fall, they returned to their own backyard, their *two* backyards actually, with their first Canadian senior Nationals at London's John Labatt Centre, and the junior world championships at the Kitchener Auditorium. The next time they'd compete at the John Labatt Centre and The Aud in the same skating year would be the 2010 Olympic season. The Labatt Centre "was jammed to the rafters" for their January homecoming, Tessa recalls, "and it was the loudest I'd ever heard at a competition. And this was the first time there were signs for us. I'd be skating around going, 'Oh! That says our names on it.'"

Tessa had hoped they would break into senior with "a top ten finish," but, responding to

Above: With Joe and Alma Moir. *Opposite:* Canadian senior Nationals competition, 2004.

an adoring crowd, they finished fourth, three spots higher than they had managed in their national junior debut. Again, Tessa and Scott saved their best for last, finishing third in the free dance ahead of the ultimate bronze medallists.

The next month, feeling they had something to prove in Kitchener because of the recent switch in training locations, they finished a strong second at the world junior championships. Scott felt the judging panel "really hammered us" for a trip in the free dance. Nevertheless, a season that had opened amid anxiety and fear was closing with a silver medal and optimism, and Tessa and Scott assumed that they would move from the junior Grand Prix to the senior circuit. But in a reversal of their leap from novice to junior three years earlier, the skaters wanted to move up and the coaches wanted to hold them back. Marina and Igor prevailed and Tessa and Scott spent the 2005–6 international season as junior skaters again.

ESSA AND SCOTT HAD SETTLED INTO LIFE IN Canton, grown accustomed to and embraced the coaching styles of Marina and Igor, and their spins and lifts coach, Johnny Johns, and their skating was thriving. They were on the ice for five hours a day, and Scott was coaching some of the younger students. Tessa, after encountering difficulties enrolling in a U.S. school because of visa issues and taking two online courses the first few months in Michigan, had enrolled at Holy Names High School in Windsor the previous January and was enjoying being back in class again. The only issue was that Holy Names students had to wear school uniforms. "So it was all about accessorizing," she laughs. Scott says he "still had some growing up to do, though. In the off-season, I was still breaking down over the Junior Worlds; I thought I'd let the team down when we really needed to skate the lights out. Marina said, 'What's wrong with you? It's

"WE HAD TO LEARN HOW TO COMPETE, BEING THE FAVOURITES. WE'D ALWAYS BEEN THE CHALLENGERS. IT'S A TOTALLY DIFFERENT FEELING BEING ON THE ICE WITH EVERYONE COMING AFTER YOU." —*Tessa*

Right: On the ice at Skate Canada, 2006.
Below: In Andorra, 2005.

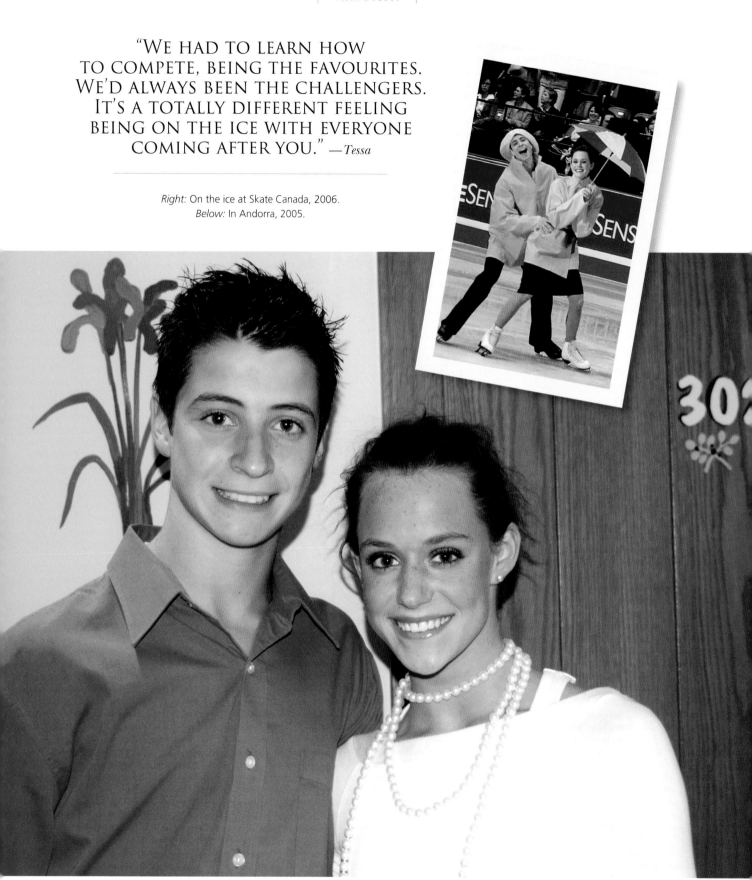

over, you have to start thinking about the future. It's time to grow up and be a man.' In her heavy accent."

Tessa is quick to defend her partner: "In our minds we had decided, 'Okay, we'll win junior Worlds this year and then we'll go to senior Worlds. But we didn't win Junior Worlds and then Marina and Igor wanted us to stay in junior, so we kind of felt we had let ourselves down. We expected more of ourselves, and it was the first time we had to deal with that kind of setback."

The young couple were used to exceeding expectations, including their own, and for part of the summer of 2005, "We thought our life was over, but it turned out it worked in our favour," Scott says. They eventually moved beyond their disappointment, and used it to fuel their motivation for another busy season. And, as the year progressed, they discovered their coaches were right in holding them back for the first time in their career.

"We had to learn how to compete, being the favourites," Tessa explains. "We'd always been the challengers. It's a totally different feeling being on the ice with everyone coming after you."

"And you have everything to lose," Scott continues. "It took a lot of getting used to. I was a lot more nervous that year but we did pretty well with it."

In fact, they went undefeated through the fall season, winning junior Grand Prix events in Montreal and Andorra within a three-week period in September and the Junior Grand Prix Final in the Czech Republic in November. And this was despite not being overly enthusiastic about the music for the free dance program. Tessa and Scott had learned from past experience that because they both put everything they have into their programs every day, they both have to like the music. But in the spring of 2005, the two coaches and the two skaters hadn't been able to come to a consensus about their music. Finally Igor said, "Time's up," and chose the music for them. Tessa and Scott never totally got the feel of the music, but it didn't prevent them from sweeping their fall events and coming into their second senior Nationals riding a tailwind.

They finished third at Nationals, but were second in both the OD and the free dance. "We thought, 'We're probably going to the Olympics because we were second in the two most important parts.' I guess that's what we went into Nationals thinking," Tessa recalls. But Skate Canada officials followed established protocol and named Dubreuil and Lauzon and silver medallists Wing and Lowe to the Olympics in Torino and the Worlds in Calgary.

"It was devastating to a sixteen-year-old," Tessa says. "Vancouver was four years away and we thought we needed to know what an Olympics is like. It was a huge disappointment and made me re-evaluate. I wasn't sure I was ready to put in another four years to get to an Olympics. But looking back it was the best thing that could have happened to us."

Just like Igor insisting that they stay at the junior level for an extra year of internationals, being passed over for the 2006 Olympic team eventually made Tessa and Scott even more determined. And Tessa now feels that had they gone to Worlds or Olympics, they would have had to move up slowly rather than using the experience and maturity of another year to make a more heralded and impressive world senior debut.

"It's funny, though, because people would ask me during the Vancouver Olympics if I was enjoying them more than the last ones," Scott laughs. "Well, yeah, I wasn't watching them in my living room!"

They still had junior Worlds in March to look forward to. And they dominated the competition that week in Lublijana, taking first in all three segments and amassing 172.57 points under the new judging system to become the first Canadian ice dancers ever to win the world junior title. In fact, Canada hadn't won a junior world championship in any discipline since 1978. Many observers felt bronze medallists Meryl Davis and Charlie White should have been second.

Meryl and Charlie, Michigan natives who had been together only a year less than Tessa and Scott, had moved from the Detroit Figure Skating Club earlier that year to work with Marina and Igor. Although they compete head-to-head and dominate their generation of ice dancers, the four skaters are friends, with Scott and Charlie particularly close. Scott and

Charlie both played competitive hockey well into their teens, and discovered by accident one day that they had played against each other in a tournament, with a bench-clearing brawl highlighting the game.

Before departing for Lublijana, Tessa and Scott had spent an eerie few weeks in Canton, as their coaches and three of the dance teams they trained closely with had all departed for the Olympics. But even that turned into a positive as Skate Canada's Marijane Stong, who had known Tessa and Scott since their very earliest competitions, came to Canton to fill the coaching void. She provided a different energy and a different set of eyes, but most importantly she introduced them to "key words."

"It's just an easy way for Tessa and I to communicate before we perform, without really talking," Scott explains.

"Something like 'knees' might really mean 'bend your knees,' or 'time' means 'we don't have anything to rush for,'" Tessa continues. "After the warmup, we talk through our whole program together and say, 'When we get to this point, we're going to think about this,' and we use our key words there. Then when we get on the ice and say those words, it clicks."

They use about fifteen of those key words, and it should come as no surprise that one is a particular favourite, for both of them: "Together."

Opposite top: With Meryl Davis and Charlie White in Andorra, 2005.
Opposite below: At Junior Worlds in Venice, 2005.
Opposite bottom and right: On the ice during competition in Andorra.

"WE WANTED IT SO BADLY. MARINA AND IGOR WANTED IT SO BADLY. WE KNEW THE NEXT STEP WAS WINNING." —*Tessa*

Chapter Four

ROAD TO GOLD

TESSA AND SCOTT WOULD OFTEN USE THE KEY WORDS "BEST IN THE WORLD" DURING PRACTICE. THAT MOTIVATED THEM TO TRAIN MORE INTENSELY THAN EVER BEFORE.

WHEN TESSA AND SCOTT WERE finally able to leave junior skating for good, as world champions, they also left behind the only season in which they had been the chased rather than the chasers.

In fall 2006, recovered from the disappointment of not being selected for the Torino Olympics and armed with two new programs, they were back to climbing their way up the ladder. Tessa was seventeen and Scott had just turned nineteen when they entered senior ranks full-time with their first Grand Prix appearance in Victoria, B.C.

Their teammates at that initial Skate Canada were the stately Canadian champions Marie-France Dubreuil and Patrice Lauzon, who had been forced to withdraw from the Olympics when Marie-France was badly injured during the competition. This season was to be their swan song in elite skating.

"They took us in and showed us the ropes," Scott says of the couple he had been gaping at in the hotel elevator at Nationals less than two years earlier. "They led by

example. They were such seasoned veterans, and they helped us all year."

"We felt supported by them," Tessa continues. "And they had a reason to be threatened by us, I think. So that's why it came as a surprise in Victoria when they were so great with us. We really felt that support. And I felt it again on tour after the 2010 Olympics because we were going in as the rookies, and Marie-France and Patrice really took us in. It wasn't like they sat down and gave us advice. It was just a feeling."

Right: Attending a banquet in 2007.
Opposite: Posing on a carousel during a photoshoot.

As Tessa and Scott expected, senior competition was a different landscape than junior. Marie-France and Patrice won Skate Canada that fall — "by a mile," Scott laughs. But by earning a silver medal in their first senior Grand Prix, Tessa and Scott created a huge splash in Victoria that sent ripples of awareness across the entire ice dancing world.

Their Original Dance, skated to "Assassination Tango," wasn't so kind to the young Canadians in their next Grand Prix event, Trophée Eric Bompard, in Paris. They were a struggling eighth in the OD, finishing fourth overall. The French event had a much stronger field, and the top two teams there went on to win the next two world championships.

Tessa recalls thinking, as she often does, that "everyone seems so much better than us."

But Scott is Tessa's alter ego when it comes to assessing the opposition. While he may sometimes get a little over-optimistic, he always sees where the teams ahead of them were vulnerable. Tessa, on the other hand, sometimes gives the opposition too much credit. She agrees that skating fans might be surprised to learn of those doubts. "Probably," she says. "Part of what we do when we step on the ice is looking confident, looking like you think you should win. That's all part of the game. It's kind of like that duck: on the surface you're calm, but inside I was very nervous."

Scott, on the other hand, looked at the three couples above them at the French Grand Prix and decided, "We can beat these guys. I didn't think that we *should* have beaten them then. They killed us. But we weren't that far off. I thought, 'We know what we have to do in order to beat these teams.'"

Opposite: With medals at Four Continents, 2007.
Right: Performing their Original Dance program in 2007.

IN JANUARY 2007 TESSA AND SCOTT FINISHED SEC-
ond at Nationals, securing the world team
berth that had eluded them the year before,
and, after winning bronze at the Four Continents championship in Colorado Springs,
headed to their first world championship in Tokyo.
Tessa and Scott finished sixth, an impressive result
by any standards. Their sixth-place finish was the
highest world championship debut by a Canadian
ice dance team in exactly forty years.

"That was huge, and we were very happy," says
Tessa, who had been hoping only for a top-ten finish. "We were the very first to skate the compulsory
dance and went in thinking, 'This is nice, trying to
advance and move up, after the year we had the year
before when we were defending, in juniors. This is a
different kind of pressure: we don't have anything to
lose, we can just go after it.' We had a good free skate,

sixth overall, and we were really pleased with it."

The difference between sixth and fifth, like
the difference between fourth and the bronze
medal, means more than just one spot. At competition, the top five couples all skate in the same
flight, warm-up group, and practice session. The
talent is better and the competition more fierce.
And judges, being only human, have more respect
and higher expectations for the final flight.

Tessa and Scott had watched the final group
during the week, and immediately after leaving the
kiss and cry, where they celebrated a remarkable
entry onto the world stage, their first thought was
all business.

"We said, 'Let's get into that last group,'"
Scott says.

And that became the target for the 2007–8
season.

Above: On the street in Japan. *Opposite:* Backstage at Worlds in Tokyo.

Figure skaters work on their new programs in the spring, starting with the selection of music. The designated Original Dance rhythm for 2007–8 was folk music, and Marina strongly suggested Tessa and Scott skate to the Russian gypsy piece "Dark Eyes." They liked the music, but were never truly at one with it. "We have never really related to folk music until we found that flamenco in the Olympic year," Scott explains. And Tessa recalls that all season they "took a lot of heat" from some judges who felt that the young couple from Canada didn't have the background to relate to a Russian dance. Never mind that they were being coached every day by

two Russians. But the program was popular with skating fans, and by the new year they were skating it well.

"We made it work, but it wasn't really us," Scott said.

The free dance, though, was entirely different. Marina had chosen Michel Legrand's powerful theme music from the classic, bittersweet 1964 movie *The Umbrellas of Cherbourg*. Both skaters loved it from the start. They rented the video in order to immerse themselves in their individual roles: a teenaged umbrella saleswoman and a young mechanic who fall in love. He is called away to war,

unaware she is carrying his baby, and although they promise to wait for each other, she marries another man who will support her. They never get back together.

"It was us," Tessa says. "It was two young kids kind of figuring out their love for each other. It was an interesting program for us because there was a storyline to follow. And with the lyrics, you have to get into those characters, rather than do your own interpretation."

"So we really had to pay attention to every little detail," Scott continues. "I really enjoyed playing a specific character. They were young kids when they met, so that's the part of the story we related to. We were seventeen and nineteen at the time, so it was easy for us to portray these characters because it was sort of what we were: naive kids who could fall in love."

While they were elevating their interpretive skills to keep in step with their new status as top-six in the world, Tessa and Scott were also hard at work on improving their lifts and spins.

"We knew we had the best footwork in the world but we wanted to make sure that all our elements were better than anyone else's," Scott says. "So we worked a lot on coming up with unique and difficult lifts, and when we put it all together as a package it really worked well."

"The couple of years before that, everyone had been harping on our lifts, saying they weren't intricate," Tessa says. "We were getting Level 4's [the highest level], but it was just never a focus for us."

Marina and Igor brought acrobats from a circus school in Montreal to Canton, where they worked with Tessa and Scott on basic lifting technique. While Tessa and Marina explained the impression they wanted to create and the rules

Above: A photoshoot with photographer Myra Klarman.
Opposite: Performing their free dance program to the theme music from *The Umbrellas of Cherbourg*.

Above: Compulsory dance in Quebec City, 2007.
Opposite: Posing for a photo in Japan.

they had to work within, the circus performers opened the skaters' eyes to a number of new creative options. And they helped Tessa and Scott learn the circus insiders' techniques and tricks.

"Traditionally we'd thought of our lifts as really muscling them up there," Scott points out. "But we learned from them that if we worked together and counterbalanced, or if we had perfect timing and got the pop, you could make the lifts work even better than just using muscle strength on them." Working with the acrobats, they practised more off the ice than on it, and it was a turning point, Tessa says. They usually only did off-ice lifts in warm-ups at competition, assuming that the major components of the lift were the speed and momentum on the ice. Now they knew differently.

They focused mainly on the Original Dance and free dance during training, and they began adding compulsory dance practice later in the summer; at that point, however, Tessa started to feel cramps in both her shins. She'd never experienced this before and had no idea why she was in pain during compulsory dance practices, but not the OD or free dance sessions.

"So much of compulsories is sustaining a knee bend and holding an edge," she said. "I was thinking it was that or maybe my skates. I really wasn't thinking much about it, I just knew that they hurt. They didn't hurt in the OD or the free dance, so I just dealt with it."

As their competitive season opened with Skate Canada in Quebec City, Tessa was coping with the inexplicable pain by taking her skates off immediately after compulsory dance practice or competition. Tessa and Scott won by more than twenty-five points for their first senior Grand Prix victory.

"Standing on the podium was cool, but we really didn't think much of it," Scott says. "We just

wanted to go there and skate well, and get the programs underneath us. Our goal was to make the Grand Prix Final in Torino."

Which they did by finishing second at the NHK Trophy competition in Japan a couple of weeks later. Tessa's legs had hurt during the compulsories, and perhaps that's why she sometimes felt that they were overmatched in the competition, despite the fact that they won two of the three segments. No matter how she was feeling inside, they were proving now on a regular basis that they could skate with the world's best. They could, but at the Grand Prix Final in Torino, they didn't, finishing fourth overall. The Final, as it's known in skaters' parlance, includes only the Original Dance and a free dance. Scott made a major mistake on the twizzle sequence in the OD and they never fully recovered. The free dance, which they had trained for longer and had felt more comfortable with from the start, was strong.

The team and their coaches were discouraged because they had hoped to use The Final as a springboard to a strong showing at Worlds. But they learned that year that it's not as important to win The Final as it is to draw something positive out of it, something to work on before the bigger event three months later.

What Scott drew out of missing the podium at the Grand Prix Final was that, despite their finish, he and Tessa were as good as, or even better than, everybody else. "We should beat them," he thought. And that's one of the key differences in their emotional makeup. "I did NOT think that," Tessa says emphatically. "I tell her we're the best every practice," Scott says.

"Which is good," Tessa finishes, "because I'm sitting there getting a bit frightened, thinking, 'We don't even deserve to be here.'"

So while Scott's competitive confidence was a boost to Tessa's competition-week doubts (for the first eight or nine years she was sick at every competition, sometimes right on the ice, then felt fine and confident), those same doubts fuelled her determination to figure out ways to get better. She brought structure and planning to Scott's enthusiasm and bravado.

The second-year seniors expected to win the Canadian championships, held in January at the Pacific Coliseum in Vancouver, and used it as a

> "I WANT TO PLEASE AND I WANT PEOPLE TO LIKE ME, BUT THAT WAS THE SEASON THAT I STARTED TO REALIZE THAT I COULDN'T WORRY ABOUT OTHER PEOPLE AND I HAD TO BE OKAY WITH GOING IN AND BEING IN A BUBBLE." —*Tessa*

Scott admits, though, that at The Final he got so excited at the prospect of being the best that he tried to hurry the process rather than taking it a day at a time "and letting the training speak for itself, the skating speak for itself." It was an important lesson.

Tessa, too, was going through some self-discovery at the time. While Scott got along with the male skaters, despite finding the dressing room far too silent before a competition, Tessa had been taking it personally when the female skaters wouldn't talk to her, or were outright rude to her, in the dressing room. She didn't recognize that it was all part of the high-octane competitive atmosphere.

"I want to please and I want people to like me," she explains, "but that was *the* season that I started to realize that I couldn't worry about other people and I had to be okay with going in and being in a bubble." Again, it was a lesson, which would pay off in the future.

virtual tune-up for the Four Continents competition and Worlds. It was more of a coronation than a competition, and they beat the silver medallists by nearly thirty-five points.

In a bit of a role reversal, Tessa was the one who was envisioning victory over the best couples in the world in Vancouver: "I said to Scott many times, 'This is our rink. We're going to win Nationals here and then we're going to the Olympics.'"

But the Olympics were twenty-four months away, while Four Continents was the next hurdle. They won their first Four Continents competition, defeating Meryl Davis and Charlie White handily. Marina, who coaches both pairs, used a variety of psychological tricks and coaching techniques, as she always has done in the name of teaching her students to flourish under varied circumstances. For instance, she floods the rink surface only twice in the twelve-hour day at Canton, which helps dancers deal with poor ice conditions, especially in the latter, rutted rounds of compulsories. And while

Above: Performing the compulsory dance during the NHK Trophy in Japan, 2007.
Opposite: A break during a photoshoot for *Hello! Canada* magazine.

Tessa and Scott didn't skate well at The Final, Marina felt that at least Scott had learned not to get over-excited when he feels confident. And at Four Continents and Nationals, knowing that Tessa and Scott weren't in much danger of losing, she started to mess with their minds, trying to get them ready for any kind of disruption.

When Tessa and Scott began using key words at that competition, saying, "Let's really enjoy this spot," she'd interrupt, agitated, and say "NO!", implying that they really had to push through that segment of the program. She was simply trying to throw them off their game because, as she repeatedly said, "You have to learn to compete under any conditions."

Tessa and Scott had no idea what conditions would be like for them at their second Worlds, in Gothenburg, Sweden. They'd had an excellent debut at sixth the previous year, but they were hoping there would be no repeat of the Grand Prix Final.

"We were thinking we weren't at our best and we finished fourth at Final, so let's skate our best and skate for a medal," Tessa recalls. "Just our second year and we're fighting for a medal."

Scott thought they were as good as any of

Opposite: Performing the free dance at Four Continents, 2008.
Top: Gold medal win at Four Continents.
Bottom: With coach Marina Zoueva.

the top teams, but there was Tessa's nagging shin problem, which was compounded by the fact that practices for the original dance and compulsories, the pain-causing culprit, were held together. That meant entire practices of agony until the compulsories were over. A month earlier, Tessa had started working with physiotherapist Mary Brannagan in Tecumseh, a suburb of Windsor. She treated Tessa's shins with fascial release techniques which diminished the pain. But the effects of the treatment did not last. "As soon as I skated I would be in agony again." Tessa says.

"The compulsory pattern was the Argentine Tango, and after the first half pattern they would start to burn," she recalls. "I told someone in my family, 'Just so you know when you're watching me skate: after the first half I'm dying and there's another round and a half to go.'"

But Tessa's skating, and her face, didn't betray the pain she was enduring, and they delivered an excellent Argentine, finishing a shocking second to the French team.

After an exemplary compulsory, Tessa and Scott also turned in a terrific Original Dance until the dying seconds, when she did one too few rotations in the twizzles. They were hit hard by the judges and dropped to third.

"We'd learned from The Final that we needed to go out and do what we do at home, not get too excited," Tessa said. "It was a great skate until the end and I was so mad at myself afterwards. I felt guilty, I kind of felt like I let the team down. But Scott's so good about that."

"We know it's a team," Scott replies. "I could easily have lost count on my twizzles too. We don't get mad at each other, it doesn't make sense. You do a good skate together, you do a bad skate together. I think in ice dance that applies more than in any other discipline because you're always holding on, always touching each other."

"We hear teams yelling and swearing at each other all the time," Tessa says. "We've never said so much as 'shut up' to one another. We have such great respect for each other, and I think because we never started down that path of blaming or name-calling, we didn't get into the pattern."

Tessa and Scott were determined to regain the spot they had dropped with the OD, and armed with a free dance they'd loved since they heard the opening notes, they did exactly that. It was the best they ever skated "Umbrellas."

"It didn't even feel like we were skating out there," Scott recalls. "Usually we have to work really hard in that free dance, but it started and the next second it was over. I always chase that feeling."

Opposite: Original dance at Worlds in Sweden.
Left: (top) During practice; *(bottom)* A break after competition.

"IT DIDN'T EVEN FEEL LIKE WE WERE SKATING OUT THERE. USUALLY WE HAVE TO WORK REALLY HARD IN THAT FREE DANCE, BUT IT STARTED AND THE NEXT SECOND IT WAS OVER. I ALWAYS CHASE THAT FEELING." —*Scott*

They were so excited with how they had skated under pressure that they bounced around the kiss and cry and weren't concerned about the actual placement. "Then it came up on the big screen and we could actually see the Ordinal '1' for free dance," Tessa said. "It was the coolest. We hugged each other for the longest time."

The memory of which makes Scott laugh warmly: "When Tessa gets really excited, she does this thing between a laugh and a cry. It's the best. Usually I'm hugging her at that point and it's so awesome. That was the first hug-laugh, I remember. She was just so happy."

And Igor turned to them and said, "You won the free dance! You're free dance world champions."

"Standing on the podium, we were excited to be world silver medallists, but I didn't associate it with being second in the world," Scott recalls. "I thought, 'Oh *yeah*, this is the biggest competition of the year, and we rocked it. We could at least sense that we could be the best. I remember saying to my mom, 'I never want to lose a competition ever again.'"

With the silver medal — and with the unscripted light brush-kiss at the end of the free dance, their first on-ice contact of that kind of intimacy — all of Canada seemed to suddenly discover Tessa Virtue and Scott Moir. Canadians put them on their Olympic radar and many of them assumed that they were a romantic couple. The dancers themselves consider that a compliment because it means they're selling their programs well.

"I understand," Tessa smiles, "because when I see movies I'm feeling, 'Oh, but they should be together!'"

Their impressive surge to the silver medal marked the first time in forty-seven years that

Canadian ice dancers had medalled as early as their second Worlds, and Tessa and Scott felt they were perfectly positioned for the Olympics. They were the best free dancers in the world, but didn't have to hang onto a world title for the better part of two years. They were hoping, bordering on believing, that they'd win the 2009 Worlds, come into Vancouver on a roll, and win the Olympics.

"We were on track," Tessa says. "We knew we needed to work hard that fall to be the best."

But as Tessa's shins would angrily remind her, sometimes you can work *too* hard.

Just one step removed from the top of the podium, Tessa and Scott knew they could be world champions in 2009, and, by extension, Olympic champions in 2010. They'd often use "Best in the World" as their key words in practice. That motivated them to a training intensity they'd never reached before. "In retrospect," Tessa smiles, "we got a little bit crazy, I think. We wanted it so badly. Marina and Igor wanted it so badly. We knew the next step was winning."

Opposite: Performing compulsory dance during Worlds, 2008. *Above*: Tessa and Scott on their way to a charity dinner.

"WE WERE ON TRACK. WE KNEW WE NEEDED
TO WORK HARD THAT FALL TO BE THE BEST." —*Tessa*

They started spending between ten and thirteen hours per day at the Canton rink, with as many as eight of those hours on the ice. Tessa was also lifting weights and working out five days a week. She put on five pounds of muscle and lost two pounds of fat in four weeks. Scott was spending more time than previously in off-ice dance sessions and training at the barre. They had, in essence, doubled their training from any other summer and were happy to do so, but they were overdoing it.

"We felt every fourteen-hour day makes you a world champion,'" Scott explains.

The couple spent hours and hours together off the ice, working again with the acrobats from Montreal and experimenting on their own with new lifts and positions. They had decided to institute new lifts for the 2008–9 season, with as much innovation and degree of difficulty as they could. Normally they would have recycled from previous programs at least some of the three lifts, plus a creative lift (with no level attached to it) required for the free dance.

With that in mind, one morning that summer Marina brought a ballet magazine into the arena and flipped it open to a picture of a ballerina, arms spread, balanced on one knee on the back of her partner, who was bent over in a squat position. None of them had any idea at the time that this was the beginning of one of the most memorable moves in Canadian ice dancing history.

"She said, 'I think you can do this,'" Tessa recalls. "We were thinking 'You're crazy, that's never going to happen.' We really couldn't see how the mechanics of it worked, where her weight was centred. We tried it off the ice, and it was hard."

"And on the ice, it was scary," says Scott.

In the illustration, the man's feet were pointed straight ahead, where Scott's would have to be splayed sideways so he could glide. It was hard to simulate off ice because they didn't have the momentum they would on ice. They also had to find the right position for Tessa to step up onto Scott's back, and make sure she didn't cut him. They had to work out whether she was going to

Above left: Practice in Korea.
Above right: At the rink in Canton, Michigan.
Opposite: "The Goose."

enter the lift skating forwards or backwards, how far Scott would bend over, how much weight she could exert with her right skate, which would be in Scott's thigh, and how much pressure her right knee could exert on his back.

It took several exasperating months, but they finally found a workable version of the lift people had started calling the Eagle, because Tessa looked as if she were flying. But that sounded too American for a Canadian couple, so they eventually renamed it The Goose, in honour of one of Canada's national symbols.

Marina told them later that she never thought they would get it, but she wasn't taking

into account the very nature of their partnership: they are competitive about everything and they never give up. And how early in their careers in Kitchener-Waterloo, they had often been challenged to attempt hyper-difficult moves.

"The other part was that we knew we had something different, which is hard to find with the rules," Scott explains. "And we needed to get it in order to be different."

They inserted The Goose into their new free dance, which was skated to two songs by Pink Floyd, a drastic departure for them. They knew that in the following year, the Olympic season,

they'd be returning to their forte — something more classical and romantic — and wanted to show that they could skate to a variety of musical genres.

"Pink Floyd took us in another direction, but we also needed to set ourselves up to win," Tessa said. "So it was the balance of 'how hard do we push it this year without playing it safe, but still put ourselves in gold medal position?'"

Tessa and Scott loved the Pink Floyd program, but were never able to skate it to its full potential. Because of all the summer skating and off-ice work, both of Tessa's shins were quickly turning into ovens of pain.

They only practised sections of their compulsory dances, thinking that was the source of Tessa's severe leg cramping. But as the summer progressed, so did the pain, no matter what kind of skating they were doing, which she could endure for even shorter periods. "I always felt like I had to take my skates off," Tessa says, wincing at the memory. "The anterior muscle, which runs along the shin bone, was on fire. By September we couldn't make it through the programs. I could skate for maybe thirty seconds and I would have to stop: my legs would cramp, give out, and I'd lose feeling down into my feet. I'd have drop-foot, where your foot kind of just clumps because your shin doesn't work."

At first doctors thought it was shin splints, but they eventually ruled that out. Stress fractures were also ruled out. Over the summer Tessa visited four doctors. Some suggested rest; others suggested pushing through the pain. Tessa followed every suggestion but the pain just kept getting worse. So Tessa and Scott were getting frustrated and a little anxious.

"I would skate for thirty seconds and then it looked from the outside like I'd give up," says

Above: (left to right) Tessa, Joannie Rochette, Miki Ando, and Mao Asada.
Opposite: Tessa and Scott share a quiet moment on the ice during Nationals in 2009.

Tessa, the woman who never gives up. "This is the year we're supposed to be winning everything, setting ourselves up to be Olympic champions. This is the year for us and we can't even make it through a minute of our program."

While they were doing small segments of programs, as much as Tessa could stand, they weren't letting anyone, even their training mates in Canton, know the depth of her severe pain. For one thing, they didn't know what it was, and, for another, if judges found out about the injury, there was a chance they would expect a lower level of skating, which could affect the neutrality of their judging.

"They look for you to be weak rather than look for you to be strong," Scott explains.

Finally, just before they left for a national team training camp in Vancouver in September, Tessa was tested for chronic exertional compartment syndrome, a condition related to muscle overuse. A few days later, the results came back positive.

"The problem was that the tissue around my muscle was tight and the muscles couldn't expand when I exerted myself," Tessa explains. "Then the blood flow is limited and all the waste and toxins are stuck in there."

Tessa visited Skate Canada's Dr. Julia Alleyne, who explained that her options were to have surgery, which might or might not work, or to retire, something Tessa wouldn't dream of. So surgery it was.

"The surgery idea was kind of good news," says Tessa, who could barely walk by then. "Part of me was happy that something could be done about it. The other part of me was already starting to calculate, 'How long before I can get back?' The injury isn't that uncommon, but doctors don't know that much about it. And every case is different. After I talked to Dr. Julia, I had a little moment of crying. Then I called Scott, and then Marina and Igor."

"We all felt the same way," Scott continues. "At least we knew. It was weird that nobody knew what it was for so long."

On October 2, 2008, Dr. Kevin Willits of London's world-famous Fowler Kennedy Sport Medicine Clinic performed the four-hour surgery. He made two pairs of two-inch vertical — not circular as widely reported — incisions in each leg about four inches below the knee, and cut through the tissue around Tessa's shin muscle so the muscle had room to expand and contract. Over time, the scars healed astonishingly well, although she does have a slight bulging above the ankle on both legs.

Tessa recuperated at home in London, under strong pain medication, and says she lost "all my muscle" within two weeks.

She and Scott knew they'd be missing their first Grand Prix assignment, Skate Canada, but hoped they would be ready to compete for the NHK Trophy in November. But every compartment syndrome case is different, and there hadn't been

Opposite: Compulsory dance at Four Continents in Vancouver, 2009.
Left: With coaches Igor Shpilband and Marina Zoueva.

many examples to draw upon. It turned out Tessa wasn't able to get back on skates for two full months. She required intense physiotherapy to build up her strength and to learn how to walk again. She had to increase her physical activity gradually, which was difficult emotionally because she wanted to jump right back into high-level training.

Scott, meanwhile, was in Canton, running through their programs on the ice by himself and working harder in the gym than he ever had. They were hoping Tessa would be ready for NHK, but when that deadline came and went he worried that they might also miss the National championships in early January.

In early December Scott met Tessa at London's Kinsmen Arena for her "first baby steps" on the ice. She was able to skate for only about ten minutes, "kind of walking at first. I felt like a CanSkate [beginner] skater."

Preferring to avoid the scrutiny in Canton, they remained in London for another two weeks, adding a couple of minutes of skating every day, basically just holding hands and stroking together around the ice. When they returned to their Michigan training base, they were up to half an hour of stroking per day, but hadn't practised any segments of their programs. And Nationals were just three weeks away.

But the worst development was something only they knew about, and their voices still crack when they try to describe it.

"We didn't talk," they say, in perfect unison.

Much is made of how long Tessa and Scott have been together, but the corollary is just how little of their lives they've spent apart. They've known each other since they were six and eight, teamed up at eight and ten years old, and for years had spent eight hours or more per day together with only two weeks off per year. They didn't know any other situation except "together."

But during Tessa's recovery time — the longest they'd ever spent apart — they weren't in regular communication with each other. It was complicated but, essentially, they were protecting each other: she didn't want to unload her troubles on him, and he didn't want to rub it in that he was on the ice every day. When they got back together, though, they realized they'd made a horrible mistake.

"That was the worst time for our relationship, and unfortunately it was matched up with the worst time of our skating career," Tessa says, wincing. "For twelve years, we didn't even have to form full sentences to understand each other. And then we spent all that time apart and we weren't even talking."

"It was like we grew apart so much in those two months," Scott adds. "That was a whole part of it that we didn't expect. We had to learn how to get along and try to support each other. It was really quite strange."

Tessa had to quickly relearn the programs, now more fully evolved, while Scott also had to make adjustments. Skating alone, he had turned some of the segments into virtual solos, and he had to relearn them with a partner beside him. And there were constant disappointments, because a good training day would give them optimism that Tessa's leg problems were over, then "the very next day I'd be crying at the boards because I couldn't do anything with the pain."

Opposite: Performing the Viennese Waltz during compulsory dance at Canadian championships.

In January, Tessa had started seeing Mary Brannagan again for post-operative physiotherapy, which emphasized fascial release and deep leg massage. She would continue regular treatment right through the Olympic season, including the two weeks of the Vancouver Games. For the first few months the massage therapy treatments were quite painful, the worst part being when Mary worked through the scar tissues.

"And I also had to deal with the persistent numbness between the scars," Tessa recalls with a grimace. "The most frustrating part was feeling better after the treatments with Mary and then walking for five minutes and feeling pain or, worse, skating for just two minutes, feeling unbearable pain and having to stop."

They trained the programs in segments, and in a period when they'd normally be doing two run-throughs per day, they managed only one complete run-through before the Canadian championships. And the next day Tessa was in so much pain she couldn't walk.

The compulsory dance for the Canadian championships was the Viennese Waltz, of which they had done just one pass all year. Essentially, their entire training for it consisted of the five-minute warm-up at Nationals.

"We were just trying to get through it without embarrassing ourselves," Tessa says. "I felt sick about it."

But they did get through it, and also their demanding quick Original Dance. They had become realistic about their difficult Pink Floyd free dance — "We loved that program," Scott says — and removed a few interesting steps to make it easier on Tessa's legs. They won the competition without severe challenge, an important step in their recovery process, but the cost was more than a week of lost training in order for Tessa's shins to fully recover. They weren't able to train much before heading to Four Continents in Vancouver, where they were to face Meryl Davis and Charlie White, who'd been enjoying a breakthrough season.

In hindsight, Tessa and Scott had had almost no training, and so shouldn't have worried about their actual results for the rest of the season. But they are ultra-competitive, and had convinced themselves they needed to win because they were ranked second in the world and because Four Continents would set a tone for how they felt about the Pacific Coliseum, where the Olympics would be held a year later. They got through the relatively easy Finn Step compulsory, weren't in good enough physical shape to really push their Original Dance program but still won the segment, then lost the free dance, and the gold medal, to Meryl and Charlie.

"Looking back, we were just lucky and happy to make it to the end, really," Scott recalls. "When we started the last part, which is supposed to be the part with the most energy and the most excitement, we were just dog-tired. My skates were stuck to the ice, and I couldn't move. We were doing what we call July run-throughs with 8,000 people there."

Tessa felt that they were letting people down with their performances, and was also feeling a bit guilty that she was saying to the public that she felt great when in reality she was experiencing great pain most days.

"We didn't want to lie," she explains. "But we needed to say that everything was fine to believe and to be able to step on the ice and actually compete. Part of it was that, unfortunately, kind of like in the NHL, you don't say you're injured because they [the judges] come after you and we already had enough going against us."

Competing at Four Continents cost them another week of hard training for the Worlds, which were held in Los Angeles, but, ever optimistic, they felt they could still win. Their Paso Doble compulsories were strong, even though they hadn't made it through the necessary three patterns in one try, and they had immense confidence in their Pink Floyd free dance. At Worlds, they skated better compulsories than they had the previous two competitions and were third, despite Tessa "dying" after the first pattern. In the Original Dance, Scott "mucked up the twizzles ten seconds in," and they "were pretty shaky for the rest of the program." Ironically, the twizzles are individual elements, the only ones he could effectively practise on his own while Tessa was in post-op recovery in London.

They went on to skate their free dance "as well as we could under the circumstances," and had just enough to hang on to the bronze medal.

"WE LOOKED BACK AND SAID, 'WOW, WHAT A YEAR.'"—*Scott*

While they weren't happy with getting only a bronze, Scott says, "We looked back and said, 'Wow, what a year.'" And those closest to them, including Igor, felt that finishing third with their minimal, unfamiliar training patterns and with Tessa enduring such pain may have been their greatest achievement yet. Although they were still confident about the Olympics, they also had some deep apprehension because, while they had been told that Tessa should be recovered by Christmas, the season was already over and she was still experiencing pain after heavy training.

And they had a great deal of repair work to do on their relationship, which they'd put off because they had so much to do just to get their on-ice product in passable shape. They were getting along well on the ice, but were still virtual strangers off it. And that was eating away at both of them.

They did not "have a comfort zone unless we were on the ice," recalls Scott. "We were scared out of our minds that our Olympic dream was not going to be realized because of it." If they hadn't had such a history of togetherness, he says, they wouldn't have managed to skate at all in 2008–9. "So that off-season we spent a lot of time just trying to get back together, trying to become the friends that we had always been."

Friends who would go to the Olympics — and win them — just like they'd always planned.

Right: Receiving gifts for their bronze-medal win at Worlds in Los Angeles.
Below: Performing their Pink Floyd free dance program at Worlds, 2009.

"When I picked that music, I knew somehow that they would win. I knew it had total harmony for them. Every day in July 2009, I had them finish their program standing facing the Canadian flag in our rink in Canton, hands on their hearts. I know how patriotic they are. What they did, they did not do for themselves but for Canada." —*Marina Zoueva*

Chapter Five

TRIUMPH ON ICE

"WE FELT SO PROUD TO BE CANADIAN AND TO BE PART OF THESE GAMES." —*Scott*

TO ELITE ATHLETES NOTHING IS MORE THRILLing, or more pressure-packed, than an Olympics in their own country. The Winter Games always offer the potential for glory and also the burden of expectation, but both are multiplied many times over when your country is the host nation.

Tessa and Scott began thinking constantly about the Vancouver Olympics in June 2009, with the date February 22, 2010 — the night of the free dance final — etched permanently in their minds. From midsummer onward, there were increasingly energized references to Vancouver 2010.

Tessa and Scott had won a world bronze medal despite their lack of training depth, her frequent debilitating pain, and the sudden disappearance of their unique off-ice closeness. To outsiders things seemed to be back on track; only the skaters knew that their joined-at-the-hip friendship wasn't quite back yet, and that Tessa's shins were still getting in the way of Olympic-level training.

"I knew I had support from Scott and he had it from me, but we weren't expressing that," Tessa says. "Because we didn't know how to."

They had never needed to know how because it had always come so naturally. Recognizing this,

each of them began working with sports psychologists in the off-season. It was something that they had already planned to do in the Olympic season anyway, to help them organize and focus their thoughts amid all the domestic hype and pressure.

"I needed to relearn how to communicate with my partner," explains Scott, who had been trained by Suzanne Killing early in his career to analyze the team's needs. "I couldn't understand why I couldn't communicate with my partner." It would take much of the Olympic season for Tessa and Scott to restore, and then tighten even more, their longtime closeness and off-ice friendship. Outsiders, who had always assumed it was so easy for the couple to communicate, had no idea of how much of an emotional toll this was taking on both skaters. That stress was increased more by the fact that the after-effects of surgery were not abating very quickly: in fact they continued all season.

Tessa really ramped up her physiotherapy during the summer of 2009, driving the one hour from Canton to Tecumseh four or five times per week for two-hour sessions. The physiotherapy was no longer painful, but it was frustrating that the recuperative effects wouldn't last long. All season, Tessa dealt with constant disappointment: "I was

Opposite: "The Goose" at the Grand Prix Final in Tokyo, Japan, 2009.

either in too much pain to skate or I would feel better, push myself, and end up having a major setback."

There was not one competition, nor one training day, during the entire Olympic season when Tessa was completely physically healthy. Amidst the emotional upheaval and constant pain, Tessa sometimes lost confidence in her skating, and truly believed that other skaters were laughing at her in training. She had to work very hard to overcome those severe self-doubts.

Meanwhile, Igor was impressed by how she and her partner were handling their off-ice emo-

and said, "Follow me. It's time." So all three of them put their skate guards on, clomped through the arena parking lot, and sat in Marina's car. She played a segment of Gustav Mahler's Symphony no. 5, a textured classical work that is both big and subtle at the same time. Very few skaters have used it because of its elusive, almost ghostly quality, one that can be mistaken for sombreness instead of the uplifting themes Marina and her skaters heard.

"When I listened to it, I loved it," Scott said, "and I kept thinking, 'I hope Tessa likes it, I really hope Tessa likes it.'"

No worry, Tessa recalls, "because ten notes

"I LOVED IT. IT WAS ETHEREAL, WITH THE PIANO, THE VIOLINS, AND THE WHOLE ORCHESTRA. THERE ARE SO MANY LITTLE CLIMAXES. I THOUGHT THERE WERE SO MANY GOOD MOMENTS WHEN IT JUST BUILDS. I KEPT THINKING TO MYSELF, 'THIS IS OUR OLYMPIC MOMENT.'"—*Tessa*

tional estrangement. "They kept it so professional on the ice," he said. "I didn't see it affect them on the ice. The way they treated the injury and what they did the year before, they deserved a medal for that. In my experience I haven't known of any other team who could do what they did with the training they had."

Like all Canadian medal contenders, Tessa and Scott wanted to make sure that they did everything possible to help their game rise to the massive domestic expectations. For figure skaters, this included choosing musical accompaniment that was memorable, and as close to perfect as possible.

Tessa and Scott knew that Marina had a long-term plan for their Olympic music, but Marina wasn't letting on what it was. They were getting anxious because the Olympic pressure was already closing in, but they didn't know what musical vehicle they'd be using to combat it. "We actually talked about what we were going to say to her if we didn't like it," Scott reveals. "Would we be able to tell her if we didn't like it? We decided, okay, it's our Olympics, we have to tell her."

One morning Marina grabbed her car keys

in, I loved it. It was ethereal, with the piano, the violins, and the whole orchestra. There are so many little climaxes. I thought there were so many good moments when it just builds. I kept thinking to myself, 'This is our Olympic moment.'"

"We walked back into the rink," Scott continues, "and said, 'Yes.'"

And that was one of the major steps toward regaining their off-ice relationship: they were thinking the same way again and they were playing off each other's excitement. Although they had no idea what the exact choreography would be — it was the first time in her career that Tessa did not immediately plan where specific elements should go in the music — they were each already visualizing skating to Mahler in Vancouver. The work was pulling them together as it had already started to do, without them really knowing it, during the previous year's struggles.

And Marina and Igor were including their students in the creative process more than they ever had, which also helped unite them in a common purpose. "They would say, 'We want you to get from here to here, what do *you* feel comfortable

Opposite: Tessa and Scott during practice at the Skate Canada training camp, 2009.

doing?'" Tessa recalls. "And we'd come up with something and they'd make it better. So things really came from us. I mean, Marina had this vision, but the actual steps came from us, because it was just natural."

"It was *our* program," Scott says. "It's us. We made it, we helped Marina make it. She really took our greatest strengths and put them into the program."

With Igor working out the footwork and transitions, Scott listening repeatedly to the Mahler piece on his weekend drives back to Ilderton, and all four of them envisioning the same end result and contributing to the choreography, the Olympic free dance came together by July 1. Canada Day, fittingly. It was the quickest they'd ever assembled a program, which gave them more time to practise it.

The development of their Original Dance, however, was proceeding at a snail's pace. The rhythm for 2009–10 was folk dance, as it had been two years earlier, and the ISU expected that most teams would select music from their own country. Which is exactly what Tessa and Scott hoped to do. But after listening to countless cuts of Canadian music and consulting with music experts, they came up dry. Nothing they heard seemed to have an Olympic-sized dimension to it. Stymied, they

began searching elsewhere. They were looking for something strong and powerful to go with the beauty and grace of Mahler. After the skaters rejected Marina's suggestion of Mexican music, Tessa mentioned "maybe Spanish" and Marina soon handed them a stack of twenty-five flamenco CDs. Of all the cuts, they found just one song they liked: "Farrucas" by Pepe Romero.

Tessa and Scott correctly assumed that Marina wasn't sold on the flamenco, and they weren't sure themselves that it was going to work. But they loved the music, and when they applied the previous year's footwork to it, they found it was also fun to skate to: an important consideration when they would have to hear it hundreds of times before the Olympics.

To capture the feel of the flamenco, they worked with dancers who had lived and trained in Spain, and later with Chicago-based Luis Montero, one of the world's most respected Spanish dancers. But so much of what the flamenco dancers did was not transferable to the ice because they were working on a stage not much bigger than a dinner table. Tessa and Scott had so much speed and flow on the ice that they couldn't do many of the positions they were being shown. But they kept cobbling it together, regularly removing some segments and adding others.

Opposite: Performing the flamenco in November 2009. *Right:* Practising footwork.

Much of the pre-Olympic summer they focused on the free dance, and were able to do full run-throughs because Tessa's shins weren't plaguing her too much. She thought the pain had vanished for good, but when they started working Original Dance practices into their training regimen, and doing back-to-back programs, her shins got bad again. At the national team test camp in Vancouver in September, she couldn't make it through the free dance.

"We were almost a year out of surgery and a few months away from competing in the Olympic Games, and I can't get through a program," Tessa recalls. "I just lost it after that. I was crying and in pain."

"Other athletes would try to comfort us," Scott recalls, "and we would say, '*get away* from us.'"

They weren't able to train much before their first Grand Prix in Paris, and although they felt on top of their free dance, their Original Dance felt sloppy because of all the new additions. But after getting over their frustration, they gradually devised an alternative training plan. They would do a thirty-second part of their program, then take a thirty-second break, then do a ten-second part and take a short break. It was a form of interval training, and it helped build endurance into Tessa's legs. They couldn't manage full run-throughs, but at least every segment of the programs was practised.

"So when we had to do a full run-through at competition we could make it because everything was trained," Scott said. "It was completely different for us."

Under normal circumstances Tessa and Scott would have a four-week schedule before competition doing back-to-back run-throughs, with only a five-minute rest, every day for a week, then follow with a week of easier training. Then they'd repeat the cycle. Four months out from the Games, however, they were doing three run-throughs in a week at most, although the interval training was really helping.

Right: Leaving the ice after a session at Skate Canada training camp in Vancouver, B.C., September 2009.

But as Kate Virtue was driving her daughter to the airport for the flight to the Grand Prix in Paris, Tessa began crying uncontrollably, and said her legs were hurting so badly she probably couldn't make it through the programs.

"Why are we going, then? Why are we doing this?" Kate asked.

"Because I have to get to the Olympics!" Tessa answered.

At Trophée Eric Bompard, the compulsories and OD are combined into a single day, which Tessa knew would be the hardest challenge she would face all season. They hadn't yet completed a run-through of the Golden Waltz, the difficult compulsory selection, but had become accustomed to competing without enough training, so the compulsories went well. They were also determined to skate well in practice sessions so that judges in attendance would be prepared to award them the scores between nine and ten points they'd need in components to win the Games. They won all three segments in Paris to capture their first Grand Prix in nearly two years, and Tessa came away knowing that while there was still pain, she could manage three programs in two days, boosting her confidence.

Enjoying their free dance immensely and pulling on the same oar to get their OD in shape, Tessa and Scott were as unified on the ice as they'd ever been. It was spilling over into their off-ice relationship, but that was still very much a work in progress. They weren't really getting along off the ice and weren't talking to each other, outside of skating-related discussions. There is always pressure on ice dancers to be seen together away from the rink in order to create the impression that they're a true, inseparable partnership. That pressure became particularly evident to Tessa and Scott once they reached senior ranks.

"We had people say to us, 'Go be seen. Go eat together, because people are watching,'" Tessa says.

"But we *are* together," Scott continues, "so we don't have to fake it."

However, a year after her surgery, Tessa and Scott still weren't together the way they had been since the early days of their partnership, and it was eating at both of them. Tessa explains that they had somehow lost the deep trust in each other they had built through so many years, and it was taking a long time to recover it. They recall that at the Paris Grand Prix they felt the pressure to be seen together greater than they ever had, likely because they did not *feel* together.

Tessa also had an effective sounding board in her physiotherapist, Mary Brannagan, who spent six hours a day in Paris working on her legs. That was financed by B2ten, a private sector program that supports Canadian Olympians, and Scott and Tessa were quick to thank that organization in media interviews during the Games. Mary "became the place I could go to talk and vent and feel comfortable. I could talk through my program with her and she had me feeling confident," Tessa says, thankfully.

In their first Grand Prix of the season, all skaters collect indirect feedback from international judges, and what the Canadians were hearing was that their free dance was impressive but that the OD needed more polishing and more character and authenticity. Before Skate Canada, five weeks later, they worked with Luis Montero again to elevate their flamenco to the next level. They could do only a light week of training after Paris so Tessa's legs could recover, but they had been expecting that. They shifted into a higher gear, still not at the training intensity they'd been at most of their careers but no longer limited to two or three program run-throughs per week.

For the Olympic season only, Skate Canada had been moved to the sixth and final spot on the Grand Prix calendar, just two weeks from The Final. It was at The Aud in Kitchener. "Most of our friends were there, and we were feeling pretty good and raring to go," Scott recalls.

The compulsory dance, "Tango Romantica," was easier on Tessa's shins than the Golden Waltz, but they hadn't done a full pattern of it until they arrived in Kitchener, and did only one run-through there in practice. But, as in Paris, they pulled it out and won the segment. They also won the OD, but Tessa "wasn't mentally in it" and stumbled three times. She says part of the problem was that in looking around the rink for friends and relatives before they skated — something she had always

"WE WERE TICKED OFF BECAUSE WE DIDN'T SKATE WELL, BUT WE WERE MORE DISAPPOINTED BECAUSE WE HAD SO MANY PEOPLE IN THE CROWD AND WANTED TO SKATE WELL FOR THEM. WE TALKED ABOUT IT AND SAID, 'LET'S JUST DO WELL IN THE FREE DANCE TOMORROW.'" —*Scott*

done, but not since her surgery — she lost focus. Scott also made a mistake in the twizzle. "That was probably the first time we had a disaster and were composed about it," Scott says. "We were ticked off because we didn't skate well, but we were more disappointed because we had so many people in the crowd and wanted to skate well for them. We talked about it and said, 'Let's just do well in the free dance tomorrow.'"

"Looking back, it was the perfect thing that could have happened to us," Tessa now says. "We needed to learn to compete under different circumstances."

"And we knew we needed to change some of that OD too," Scott says, which they eventually did. "The next day we went out and did a beautiful free dance, and we really captured the moment. We felt like the competition was a triumph because we'd

Above: Tessa and Scott listen as their marks are posted during the Skate Canada competition, 2009.

come back and really skated well. It could have been a disaster."

Instead, it was a pivotal moment in their Olympic year. Tessa had been so distressed by her stumbles in the OD that she had trouble raising the enthusiasm for the free dance. But warming up off-ice "something just clicked," and she went to the right place mentally, convinced she had to stay in a personal bubble during the rest of the year's competitions. They skated brilliantly to win by nineteen points, and one judge even gave them a ten for performance, the first ever for ice dancers under the new system.

"That was a big turning point in the off-ice relationship," Tessa now realizes. "We had to be supportive and we had to be there for each other."

Tessa was still in regular pain from her shins, but with Scott's and Mary Brannagan's help she had learned to manage her injury so that it wasn't a distraction and didn't affect her performance.

With their first two-win season on the Grand Prix, Tessa and Scott headed to December's Grand Prix Final in Tokyo feeling buoyed. Their main opposition there would be their training mates Meryl Davis and Charlie White, who had also won twice that fall and whose Bollywood-themed Original Dance was considered the best in the world that autumn. Tessa and Scott's plane from Detroit was delayed on the tarmac for five hours and eventually grounded. By the time they made it to Japan, it was the night before the Original Dance. In the opening segment, they hit a wall of fatigue partway through but performed decently.

"We were fine with it — well, not fine, exactly, because we're so competitive — but Meryl and Charlie's OD was *the* OD of the season," Tessa says. "That was their program, where the free dance felt more like our program."

Scott, meanwhile, liked the idea that with their win Meryl and Charlie might be the team other

Above: Tessa with her brother Kevin outside of Bob Evans restaurant. *Left:* The end of their free dance program at Nationals, January 2010.

Posing for a photo following the Grand Prix Final in Tokyo, Japan. *From left*, Bronze medallists Nathalie Pechalat and Fabian Bourzat of France; gold medallists Meryl Davis and Charlie White of the U.S., and silver medallists Tessa and Scott.

couples would be gunning for at the Olympics, "and we would be kind of lying in the weeds."

At The Final, the Canadians had gotten wind that many judges were starting to consider their signature lift, The Goose, illegal. It had a rotation and a quarter in Tessa's exit, rather than the limit of one turn, even though it was when she was dismounting rather than being lifted. "We looked for answers," Scott said, "because as far as we were concerned we weren't going to the Olympics to get second."

Together, they chomped at the bit to leave Japan and get back to Canton to redesign the exit from The Goose and make changes to their flamenco Original Dance. "We connected," Tessa

They blew into January's Canadian championships with mounting confidence. The Nationals were held at London's beautiful John Labatt Centre, just twenty minutes south of Ilderton, and because of the adoring hometown crowd's energy and their heavy-favourite status they treated it like a "mini-Olympics." Although "they knew every volunteer" and had some connection to nearly half the crowd, they remained in their bubble, kept mostly to themselves, and concentrated on presenting three consecutive good skates for the first time that season.

"I was starting to believe that if we had a good OD one day we wouldn't have a good free dance the next," Scott says. "But I knew I had to challenge myself to do three in a row."

"OFF THE ICE, OUR RELATIONSHIP WAS BETTER THAN IT'S EVER BEEN AND I CAME AWAY FROM THE NATIONALS FEELING THAT WE WERE GOING TO WIN THE OLYMPICS. BUT THREE DAYS LATER, WHEN I WAS CRYING AT THE RINK AND COULDN'T SKATE BECAUSE MY LEGS WERE IN PAIN, I WAS FEELING LIKE WE DIDN'T EVEN DESERVE TO BE ON THE TEAM." —*Tessa*

---

smiles. "We were talking but there was more that we weren't saying that was understood. It was the first time that we had felt that again."

BACK IN CANTON, TESSA AND SCOTT WENT into high gear, training more intensely than they'd been able to for the better part of two years. They worked again with Luis Montero and really grew into their flamenco characters, changed some of the side-by-side footwork with Marina and Igor's permission, elevated their speed and power, and became much more explosive in their OD presentation. Tessa was still experiencing pain in her legs, but had learned how to train around it. One day before Christmas, she was able to make it through her first double run-through of the free dance in two seasons, and she and Scott celebrated at the nearby Bob Evans Restaurant, "where a lot of my life happens," she jokes.

They skated brilliantly in all three segments, with their OD showing particular improvement after all the hard work, and won their third Canadian title. After their flamenco, Marina called them into the women's dressing room ("THAT was awkward," Scott quips) and said, 'I'm telling you the story now because you performed that program so well; but of the hundreds and hundreds of flamencos that you listened to and found only ONE that you liked, it was the one song that [her legendary pair] Gordeeva and Grinkov also chose for their flamenco.'"

"Off the ice, our relationship was better than it's ever been," Tessa says, "and I came away from the Nationals feeling that we were going to win the Olympics. But three days later, when I was crying at the rink and couldn't skate because my legs were in pain, I was feeling like we didn't even deserve to be on the team."

But through more than a year of setbacks they had learned how to recover emotionally and

physically and build their training back up slowly. They fit in one week of run-throughs, and worked on the Olympic compulsory, the Tango Romantica, with Elena Tchaikovskaya, who had helped her hall-of-fame students, Alexander Gorshkov and Lyudmila Pakhomova, invent the dance in the mid-1970s.

MEANWHILE OLYMPIC FEVER, FUELLED BY A cross-continent torch relay, was seizing Canada. One benefit of being in the U.S. and having to focus so much on Tessa's shins, training alternatives, and making it through one competition at a time was that they had too much to worry about and were never overcome by Olympic jitters. "We knew that as long as we did as much as we could that we would be happy," Scott says. "And that became the goal. I mean, you wake up every day, and you go to sleep every night, praying and dreaming about the Olympics. There's no doubt about that. But there were never any negative feelings about the Olympics."

Tessa and Scott were helped greatly in their positive approach to the pressure-packed Games by the experience of 2002 Olympic pairs champion David Pelletier, who had joined their team as an advisor, and eventually began acting in an agent capacity for the young Canadians.

"He was a critical member of our support team," Tessa says. "A wonderful mentor and a 'go-to' person for us leading into the Games. He'd been there before and knew what to expect."

Above: Waiting for their flight to Vancouver, B.C., February 11, 2010.
Right: Tessa and Scott at the Vancouver 2010 Winter Olympics Opening Ceremonies.

Right: The Opening Ceremonies of the 2010 Vancouver Olympics.
Below: With Igor, Marina, and Elena Tchaikovskaya, who helped choreograph their Tango Romantica compulsory program.

And on February 11, Tessa, Scott, and Marina flew to Vancouver.

"I was in shock in the athletes' village for the first two or three days," Tessa says. "It was overwhelming, there was so much to take in, and there are so many athletes. You're kind of unsure if you belong."

"You wanted to be up in the lounge with people, and then you wanted to be watching the athletes," Scott said. "I'm glad we went a week early for our first one because you really have to learn in the village to not get consumed with everything. It's amazing, it's the best feeling in the world to be there with the team."

Skate Canada had booked extra ice time over four days in nearby Port Moody — and Tessa and Scott had arranged for Meryl and Charlie to work out there too — but things took a turn for the worse. One day her shin pain was so bad that Tessa was having trouble breathing. Again, they took it

easy, and by the time they had their first official practice at the Pacific Coliseum, on the first day of the Games, they were back in top form. There was no one in the stands, but "the energy in the building was perfect," Tessa recalls.

They arrived at the Opening Ceremonies at BC Place and were surprised that they had to line up "for hours and hours" awaiting the athletes' parade. They both say that had they had to compete the next day they could not have taken part, but it was all worth it as they entered the stadium, with Marina beside them, proud to be representing the country that had first taken her in.

"We were in the tunnel [waiting to walk into the arena] and heard 'Canada' and the roar that went with it," Scott recalls, dropping his jaw in awe. "We were in shock. I said to Tessa in the line, 'I'm nervous because it's our country that's on display. If they don't do a great job, I'm going to feel kind of responsible.' But all the athletes kept saying all

Opposite: With Marina in Vancouver. *Above:* Athletes' parade at BC Place.
Right: In the athletes' village.

week, 'Best Games Ever, Best Games Ever.' We felt so proud to be Canadian and be a part of these Games."

"It was amazing when we first heard 'Canada' after our names back when we started skating internationally," Tessa says. "But this just felt as if we were part of something much bigger. And everyone was coming together for this. That was unbelievable. UN-believable."

It was to be one of the most memorable Winter Games ever — partly for the wrong reasons. Earlier that morning, Georgian luger Nodar Kumaritashvili had been killed in a horrific training accident at Whistler. The de facto spokesman for the Georgian athletes became Otar Japaridze, an ice dancer whom the Canadians knew. "[Nodar] went to the Games, just like we did. They're supposed to be *games*," Tessa says.

But all elite athletes are trained to shut out even the worst circumstances, and Tessa and Scott had three competition segments to prepare for.

"We were back on track off the ice, in terms of our relationship, so marching through that together was such a team thing for us, it was just like this," Tessa says, clasping her hands tightly. "We did everything together for the entire Olympics."

They had some excellent practices, but two days before the compulsories, Tessa's shins acted up and prevented them from doing a full run-through in a free dance practice attended by many judges. They became nervous.

"We knew we had to make a good first impression," Scott explains. "Tessa was talking to me and I wasn't even listening. I was zoned out — she actually had to grab my hand. And say 'Hey, hey, we're here, it's us.' And somehow, I don't know how, I snapped out of it when we got back on the ice. I was still extremely nervous. But we skated well. Marina was so happy. She said, 'You need to skate like that. Who cares about the Olympics? That was amazing.'"

It may be that any rogue nerves, which would have undermined them in competition, were flushed out that day. When the ice dancing competition opened with compulsories on Friday, February 19, Tessa and Scott hugged each other during the warm-up in a way that soon became part of their ritual. "We feel each other breathing, just to make sure that we're together," she says. Practising breathing correctly was important in Tessa's physiotherapy because it helped get oxygen to her shins more efficiently. The crowd had gone completely crazy when they were announced during warm-up, and Tessa and Scott allowed themselves to absorb that positive energy before returning to their "just-you-and-I" bubble. Halfway through their Tango Romantica, it was obvious to even the untrained eye that they were skating magnificently, and the audience began clapping so loudly that Scott kept yelling at Tessa to keep focused.

"We've never been more in tune with each other," Tessa grins. "Never been more together. It was the *best!*"

"We were ecstatic. Until we got the marks," Scott said.

"I was still happy," Tessa says. "Scott wasn't."

Scott, angry that they had finished second, was miming to the judges: "Just wait until Sunday," when the Original Dance would be held. But Tessa thought, "'We're second. We're going to win the Olympics.' I knew it. My older brother Casey was flying in that night and I told him on the phone, 'Don't worry, Case, we're going to wait to get the gold after you arrive.'"

There was a practice day Saturday, with another early-morning practice on Sunday, the day of the Original Dance. Tessa was rooming at the village with Joannie Rochette, one of the medal contenders in women's singles. At around 5:30 a.m. Sunday, while Tessa was in the washroom quietly preparing for practice,

> "WE'VE NEVER BEEN MORE IN TUNE WITH EACH OTHER. NEVER BEEN MORE TOGETHER. IT WAS THE *BEST!*" — *Tessa*
>
> "WE WERE ECSTATIC. UNTIL WE GOT THE MARKS." — *Scott*

Left: First day of Olympic competition, skating compulsory dance Tango Romantica.

Original dance skated to "Farrucas"
by Pepe Romero.

she heard a noise and thought she had woken her roommate. "Then there was a knock on the bathroom door and I walked out and I saw everyone from Skate Canada in the common room and in our room," Tessa recalls. "I was wondering what was going on when Jo walked by me to go into the washroom and said, calmly, 'My mom died.' Just like that. Benoît Lavoie [Skate Canada president] told me what happened."

Thérèse Rochette, just fifty-five, had arrived in Vancouver with her husband Normand only the day before, and had collapsed and died late Saturday night. Normand and Skate Canada officials decided to let Joannie get some sleep before telling her the unspeakable news.

"They told me to keep my usual routine, which meant doing my hair and makeup for practice," Tessa says. "So I went into the washroom with her and we were doing our makeup side-by-side. Finally I stopped and gave her her space and went to a different washroom. I just said, 'I'm so sorry,' and 'Your mom's with you.'" I was in shock. It didn't really register."

Both Tessa and Scott felt selfish that they had to practise and concentrate on their own medal pursuit when a close friend had endured such a tragedy. But it's the ability to temporarily prevent anything from distracting them from their goals that sets elite athletes apart. Joannie Rochette herself is the same way. Before leaving for practice, though, Scott automatically wondered if his own parents would be in the stands, and that's when it hit him and he broke down crying. "Jo would never get to have that. Her mom would never see her at the Games." Tessa's voice cracks when she recalls that Kate Virtue was in the stands that morning. Tessa and Scott continually squeezed each other's hand for support, and on the bus home Tessa broke down and so they talked about the situation rather than ignore it. Scott reminded Tessa that the media would want her to comment about Joannie after the OD, and Tessa said she could handle it.

Their realization of what had happened grew over the day, but as they came to the rink for the Original Dance, Tessa and Scott were ready, telling each other that their hearts were with Joannie but they had a job to do.

"And then we went out and skated our asses off," Scott says.

With Tessa flipping her gorgeous red skirt to the beat of the music and Scott in perfect Spanish character it was a sultry, sizzling, technically demanding performance — and when they finished they both yelled "Yes!" The crowd erupted, and then erupted again when the Canadians moved into first place. At home in Ontario, Paul MacIntosh was thinking that he had just seen the greatest Original Dance ever performed in competition.

IT WAS AN IMPORTANT NIGHT NOT JUST TO THE SKATERS but the overall Canadian Olympic team. The men's hockey team had been beaten that night by the U.S. and spirits were down, especially since it had become clear that Canada was not going to win the medal count as the country's Olympic program "Own the Podium" had all but promised. Yet Scott knew the second week was going to be Canada's strong point, and it was slowly emerging the country was going to win more gold medals than ever before. As it turned out, Canada won more gold medals than any other country *ever* had.

And for the first time in two years, Tessa and Scott were glad they didn't have a day off after a competition. They wanted to keep the momentum alive. Moreover, Tessa's legs were fine because she'd had time between morning practice and evening competition to undergo physiotherapy.

After morning practice on February 22, Tessa and Scott each battled their own demons. Both were engaged in positive thinking, trying to replay a successful program in their minds. But Scott kept imagining a three-turn in which Tessa's skate sliced him. Tessa was having a similar experience during physio as she played the Mahler piece over and over again on her iPod. After twenty minutes, Mary Brannagan asked her why a four-minute program was taking so long to listen to. "I can't get past this part where we mess up," she said. "It took me all day to get through the four-minute program. But then I did it several times."

"If you ever want to get to know yourself," Scott says, "try those last twelve hours before an

Olympic final. You have so much time with your own thoughts, absolutely everything that could happen goes through your mind."

Tessa and Scott were scheduled to skate third from the end, and as they stroked out to take their opening positions, Tessa said, "This is our time, we deserve this." A packed arena, and several million Canadian television fans, agreed.

"We're here, kiddo," Scott said.

"Showtime!" Tessa said, her standard response.

From the first note they were in absolute sync, capturing the haunting rises and falls of the Mahler symphony so exactly that at first the crowd was dead silent in awe. Then, as it became apparent that they were witnessing history, the spectators grew as loud as the music while Tessa and Scott, exquisite in their execution and timing, stayed completely in the "zone."

"Watching that was probably one of the most magical moments of my life," Igor says. "I felt secure. I was surprised I wasn't nervous, but I knew they

Below: Basking in their success in Vancouver. *Opposite:* "The Goose" during the Olympic free dance program.

were going to do it. I'd seen them do it a million times in practice at home. At the same time, though, I did every step with them."

Marina said that when she watched Scott and Tessa skate, she was transported away from the usual technical worries of a coach. "I was just melting," she said.

"Until the last five seconds we were perfect," Scott says, explaining that in the final, dizzying, spinning lift, with the spectators on their feet screaming and hundreds of them crying, they had come out, over Tessa's objection, facing away from the judges, not toward them.

"Thirteen years together and I have learned this lesson," Scott laughs. "When you think you're

Left: Tessa and Scott performing their free dance at the 2010 Olympic Games.
Right: On the podium during the medal ceremony.

right and Tessa thinks she's right, chances are Tessa's right. We were just looking at each other: 'Seriously, we have three great programs and the last five seconds we screwed it up?' But Marina said, 'Not a chance. That was great.'"

The judges agreed, awarding them 110.42 points, the highest of their career, and four tens in the program components. Their combined score was 221.57, nearly six points higher than Meryl Davis and Charlie White. Everyone knew they were looking at the new Olympic ice dancing champions, the youngest ever and the first from North America.

"Scott kept saying to me, 'Look at this, take this in,'" Tessa says of the pandemonium in the arena.

"We were so happy," Scott says. "You *are* thinking about the journey, how everything came together. About how much your families have helped you. About everything we've gone through, and how it was all worth it. Every second of it."

B ACK IN ILDERTON, AT A GATHERING ORGANIZED BY Carol and Paul Moir, 300 people were crammed into the Community Centre watching the free skate on three large TVs.

"My older sister Marg and I were grasping hands during the free dance, and when the marks went up, we jumped and screamed and hugged the grandpas," Carol Moir says. "It was one big hugfest, 300 of us hugging. Then we had to wait for the other two free dances. It was the longest wait. And then we did it all again."

In Waterloo, Paul MacIntosh and his wife Carolyn Allwright "were jumping around our living room like mad people." Paul had eaten a club sandwich earlier, because when he was coaching Tessa and Scott he'd had one for lunch at a novice event and they had performed well, so he kept doing it for their biggest competitions, long after they'd moved to Canton. And his lucky "Be the class of the ice" e-mails were among the handful that Tessa hadn't had blocked out during Olympic week.

In the Pacific Coliseum, Suzanne Killing-Wood, whose sixteen-month-old daughter Gracie had learned to say "Tessa" shortly before Suzanne left home "to watch Tessa and Scott win," had been amazed at the awe the audience expressed while watching her former students skate.

Left: Marina, Scott, Tessa, and Igor celebrate after hearing their scores for the free dance.

"I started crying after three seconds. I was so proud. I just kept thinking how happy they were going to feel when they finished. When they knew they had done everything they possibly could, at the right moment, in their home country in front of their friends and family."

Jordan Virtue was also crying over the long journey it had been. She was sitting with her mother in the first row on the judges' side, with the rest of the family sitting in twos around the rink.

"I was nervous after I saw Meryl and Charlie's marks," Kate Virtue recalls. "They were so high

ing, 'Thank you, guys, thank you so much. Thanks for the medals, and for being part of this with us. This is the coolest feeling.' When it actually felt real was *on* the podium when we got the medals."

As Tessa and Scott "kept bouncing around" waiting for the medal ceremony, Marina was explaining to reporters how Canadian she felt, and how she felt the same way about the Mahler program that she had about creating ethereal routines for Gordeeva and Grinkov.

"You will never design a program like this without love," Marina told the *Hamilton Spectator*.

"'O CANADA' STARTED TO PLAY AND EVERYONE STARTED TO SING. IT WAS CRAZY. I COULD FEEL SCOTT'S ENERGY AND WE JUST KEPT LOOKING AT EACH OTHER. WE BOTH SANG: THERE WAS NO MICROPHONE LUCKILY. THAT WAS THE MOST FUN I EVER HAD." — *Tessa*

and they skated better than they had all year. But when Tessa and Scott took their positions on the ice, they looked so calm and controlled I relaxed. And I wanted to savour every moment."

Alma Moir was also calm when she saw that her son and Tessa were at ease when they reached centre ice. She and Joe Moir, Danny and his girlfriend, Charlie and his wife, first cousin Cara Moir, and good friends Ron and Lynn Lee had abandoned their scattered seats for an obscured-vision spot above the kiss and cry so they could all be together.

"When I saw the marks go up, there was no time to react because Joe and I had to go down to see the kids downstairs," Alma says. "When I saw them I thought, 'Did you really just win the Olympics?'"

In the kiss and cry, Tessa said to Igor, "Oh my God, I think we're Olympic champions," and he replied that he thought she was right, although Scott didn't want to jinx it until after the final two had skated. "We were so happy," Scott says. "I just wanted to thank the audience. I remember think-

"A general love, I mean. A love for a country, and a love for music. And a love for a man and a woman doing beautiful skating."

As they headed for the podium, Tessa thought "about the number of people who have helped us in thirteen years: the people who have given up so much time and money and energy. It wasn't just us. Yes, we were the two out there who were skating, but there was so much behind us. When we were on the medal stand Scott said, 'Look, no one left the rink.' There were thousands of people there, and usually at medals there are ten people, including our parents. We had so many moments that we just looked at each other and said, 'This is it! This is what we've been dreaming of.' We'd already talked a little bit about just having fun and forgetting to stand properly, forget that the cameras would be on us. I think I said, 'Can I hold your hand?' Then 'O Canada' started to play and everyone started to sing. It was crazy. I could feel Scott's energy and we just kept looking at each other. We both sang: there was no microphone luckily. That was the most fun I've ever had."

Opposite: Tessa and Scott celebrate on the podium after winning the gold medal in ice dance.

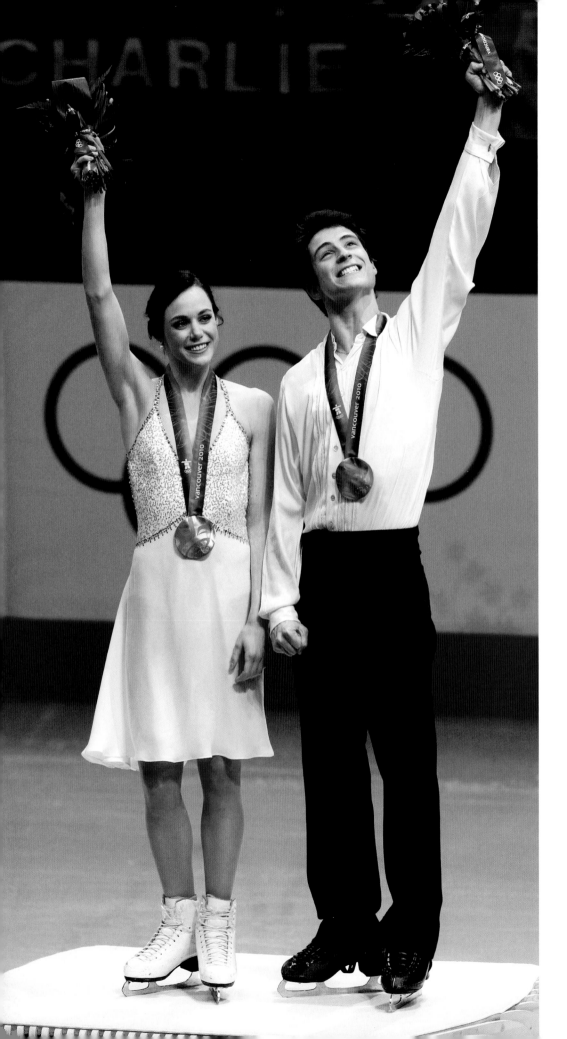

Opposite: (clockwise from top) Approaching the stands after the medal ceremony; Tessa smiling after the medal ceremony; Scott hugging his brothers Danny and Charlie in the stands.
Left: On the podium after the presentation of the medals.

vancouver 2010

2010

After media interviews, Tessa had her name drawn for doping control. The forty-five minutes of testing took her away from Scott and her family, causing her an eerie feeling of separation in the greatest hour of her young life. To fill the time Scott went out to the empty arena. "I just snuck out there and I kissed the rings, and suddenly the five people still in there broke out cheering." They were maintenance staff, and Scott climbed into the stands to have his picture taken with them.

After a celebration with their families at a downtown restaurant, they did interviews until 8 a.m., had ninety minutes of sleep — Scott couldn't nod off, so called all his buddies and his uncle — then spent most of the next day doing more media interviews. They spent the rest of the time together, enjoying the Olympics, cheering for the hockey teams, and attending Joannie Rochette's

Opposite: Celebrating on the podium.
Above: On the ice with the Canadian flag.
Below: Scott in the empty arena after the gold medal win.

Clockwise from top: Media interviews; *(left to right)* Joe, Alma, Scott, Charlie, and Danny Moir celebrating at a downtown restaurant; Tessa celebrating with brother Kevin; with medals at a press conference. *Opposite:* Tessa and Scott attend men's hockey events during the Games.

Above: Posing with coaches Igor and Marina and fellow skaters Charlie White and Meryl Davis during the Games.
Below: Scott is greeted on the tarmac by Alma and Joe Moir after he and Tessa arrive home from the Games,
March 2010. *Opposite:* Tessa and Scott entering London Airport.

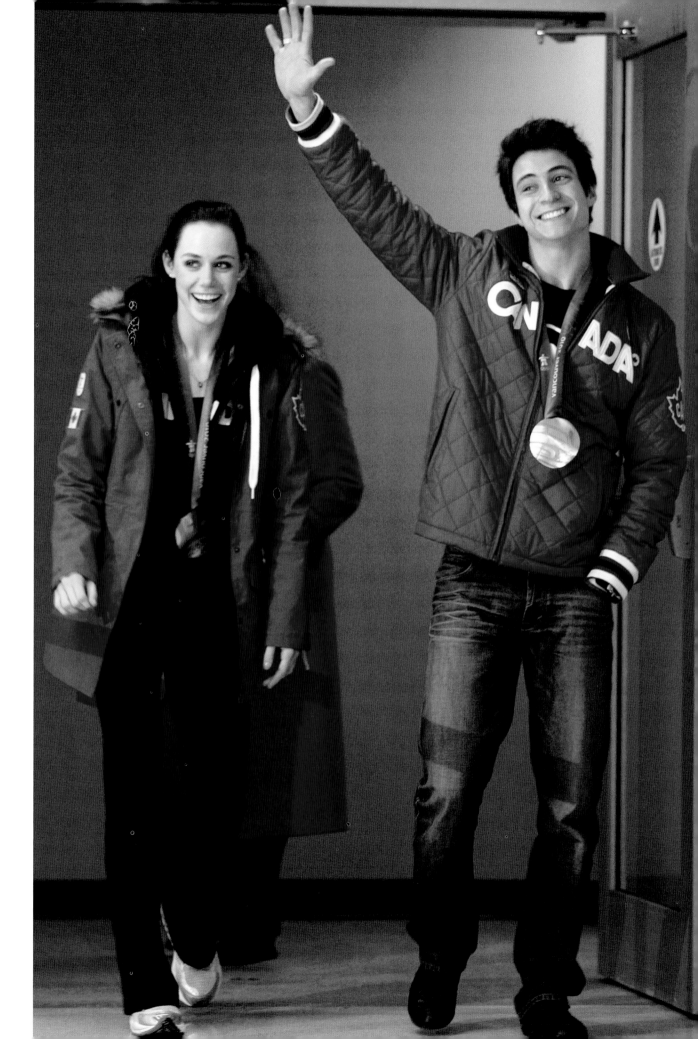

inspiring bronze medal triumph over her unfathomable grief. They celebrated with the rest of the country when Sidney Crosby's overtime goal, the last moment of the actual Games, gave Canada its record fourteenth gold medal.

Not once in that afterglow did they even consider skipping the following month's world championships in Turin. They had decided in January that they wanted to win the Olympics, then the Worlds, because they'd never had that title. But each would eventually discover why the last three Olympic ice dance champions had not attended the ensuing Worlds. Back in Canton, Tessa found that her body was tired from two years of injury and worry, and because she hadn't had time for as much physiotherapy her shins were "awful." After all the Olympic adrenalin it was hard to get motivated for those seven-hour days at the training rink. Scott, meanwhile, was excited during training, but when they got to Turin their viewpoints flipped. He found that while he had his usual competition nerves, he was without his competitive edge, while Tessa was in full competition mode.

However, they skated well in the Golden Waltz compulsory, and then set a world record with 70.27 points in the Original Dance. That was despite being informed before the warm-up, through Skate Canada and Marina, that the judging panel was likely going to declare their final lift illegal, which would cost them two points. "We decided not to think about it until we got there and just winged it," Tessa says, "and I don't even remember what we did." But they avoided the deduction that would have cost them the world title. Scott had trouble with a twizzle during the free dance, and Meryl and Charlie won the segment to finish second. "But technically it was good, we weren't cautious, and I think it was really a good way to end the season," Scott says.

Right: On the ice during the exhibition gala at the World Championships in Turin, Italy, March 2010.

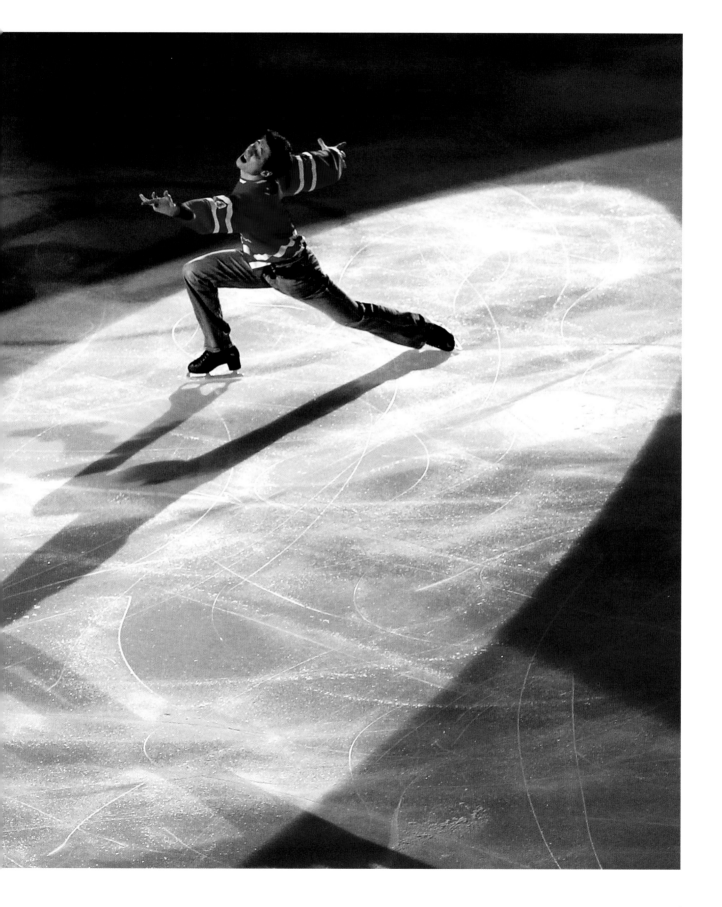

So, while there had never been an Olympic ice dance champion from North America and no world champion before 2003, Canadians had now won both the Worlds and Olympics in the same season with Americans right behind them in both. The power base had clearly shifted, although Tessa and Scott weren't dwelling on that.

"Ice dancing should be a North American force," Scott says flatly.

"It comes back to being the eight- and ten-year-olds that were always the smallest and youngest team," Tessa adds. "We were always battling with that, so battling as North Americans was just part of the story. No one told us we couldn't do it."

"ICE DANCING SHOULD BE A NORTH AMERICAN FORCE."—*Scott*

Left: Final moments of the free dance program at the Worlds, 2010.
Opposite: On the podium at the Worlds.

Tessa and Scott are struck by the contrast between the photos on their podium at Worlds and those from the Olympics. In Vancouver, they were joyous and full of abandon while in Turin they were visibly tired. It had been a long, emotionally exhausting battle back from injury and off-ice estrangement. But they had captured hearts across Canada, had elevated ice dancing far beyond what it had ever been in the country, and had proven that they were correct when they left Ilderton to pursue their Olympic dream.

"When they finished their Olympic free dance after having been through so much, I was thinking that there were these eight- and ten-year-olds who set a goal, and they achieved it," Kate Virtue marvels. "Who does that in life?"

Tessa and Scott had done it. And it was time to take their ultimate achievement back to its roots.

"WE WERE DOING
OUR OWN THINGS
IN OUR OWN WAY,
AND IT WAS POWERFUL." —*Tessa*

Tessa and Scott on the ice during a practice in Canton, Michigan.
Opposite: With their gold medals in Ilderton, Ontario.

Chapter Six

GOING THEIR OWN WAY

AFTER THEIR VICTORY IN VANCOUVER, TESSA AND SCOTT TOOK
A BREAK TO REGROUP, HEAL, AND FOCUS ON IMPROVING THEIR
ARTISTRY, ATHLETICISM, AND TECHNIQUE BEFORE HEADING
INTO THEIR SECOND OLYMPICS IN SOCHI.

AS FAR BACK AS HE CAN REMEMBER, SCOTT has always loved the Ilderton Fair Parade, which kicks off the Ilderton Fair, one of the oldest and most honoured agricultural fairs in Ontario. When he was young, he'd thrill to the floats and marchers proceeding slowly from the post office down Ilderton Road and into the fairgrounds near his family home. Eventually, in recognition of their skating achievements, he and Tessa appeared in the parade.

"We used to joke that Scott thought the Ilderton Fair was a national holiday," Tessa laughs.

"I still do," Scott laughs back.

Because of training for the Grand Prix circuit, Scott didn't make it home to fair weekend for two or three years. But on June 12, 2010, he and Tessa were honoured with their own procession through town. And it meant more to both of them than even the venerable Ilderton Fair Parade.

As they rode toward the arena in a horse-drawn carriage, preceded by torch bearers, and by their families in a horse-drawn carriage of their own, the streets were lined several-deep with cheering well-wishers, most of them clad in bright, patriotic red. The Canadian flag was everywhere, kids wore shirts bearing the Olympic slogan "Believe!," and one person even displayed a three-foot-tall wooden cut-out of a Canada goose with a "The Goose is Golden" sign on their lawn in honour of Tessa and Scott's legendary lift. There were 3,000 friends and fans crammed inside the arena for ceremonies, and another 1,000 overflow tickets sold for the adjacent curling rink — a turnout at least double the official population of Ilderton.

"The support they showed us was unbelievable," Tessa marvels. "And what was cool was that everyone had been there from the beginning. That's where it started for Scott and me — in that rink. We felt that support from the very beginning, when we were heading off to sectional championships, not just for the Olympics."

And something extraordinary happened to a number of celebrants, including Tessa and Scott, as they watched a video of the gold medal free dance on the giant arena screens. They had all believed that February 22 would always stand without

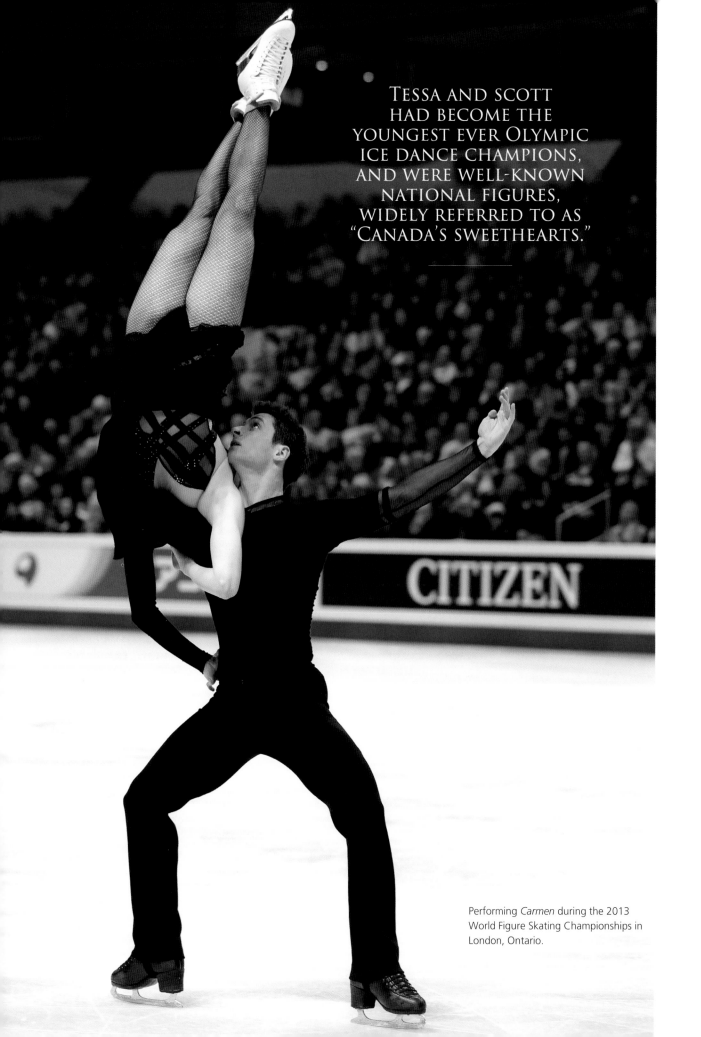

TESSA AND SCOTT
HAD BECOME THE
YOUNGEST EVER OLYMPIC
ICE DANCE CHAMPIONS,
AND WERE WELL-KNOWN
NATIONAL FIGURES,
WIDELY REFERRED TO AS
"CANADA'S SWEETHEARTS."

Performing *Carmen* during the 2013
World Figure Skating Championships in
London, Ontario.

equal, but here they were eighty days later, with the same feelings of pride, thankfulness, and excitement overcoming them just as forcefully.

"We thought we'd never feel that way again, but we all relived it on that weekend," said their first coach, Carol Moir. Her twin sister Alma, Scott's mother, echoed that emotion, turning to Kate Virtue and whispering, "I can't believe how nervous I am . . . and I know how it all turns out!" There was also a replay of the video of a packed Ilderton Community Centre on February 22. Watching the wild victory celebration, Tessa said, "Part of me kind of wishes I was there that night."

At the time, Tessa and Scott had said publicly only that they were returning for the 2010–11 season, and would decide on their future skating after that. One attraction of their return to the amateur ranks was that, the very month of the Ilderton parade, the ISU had made an expected change to ice dancing. The compulsory dance would be dropped to bring ice dance down to two segments — the short dance and the free dance — and therefore in line with the other three skating disciplines.

Most elite ice dancers, including Tessa and Scott, applauded the change because preparing for compulsory dances had required sixty to ninety minutes per day during peak training periods.

"Now you can spend more time artistically," Tessa said. And that was important to the young Olympic champions, who wanted to help steer ice dancing in a healthy direction while pushing its boundaries. When they talked artistry, they saw it not as separate from skating's athletic and technical components but as part of an integrated whole, each component blending seamlessly into the other.

Their Mahler free dance had demonstrated that kind of almost invisible marriage between the artistic and the technical, but they felt it could be stretched even farther.

One complication was that with the dropping of compulsory dances, some of the rules and requirements were actually tightened, especially in the new short dance, to guard against the "art" component overshadowing the "sport" component. But it did potentially limit some of the creativity of the elite teams who wished to push the envelope.

As Tessa and Scott returned to their home away from home at the Arctic Edge Skating Club in Canton, the long runway stretching toward the 2014 Olympics in Sochi, Russia, looked much different for them than it had four years earlier when the Vancouver Games loomed at the end of the tarmac.

They had become the youngest ever Olympic ice dance champions, and were well-known national figures, widely referred to as "Canada's sweethearts," with all the attendant publicity and expectations. It was an environment for which no one could fully prepare them. "There was a lot of growing up," recalls Scott, who, at the time, was uncomfortable with so much public attention. They had to figure out their value in the corporate marketplace, and to weave a path through multiple responsibilities to sponsors, scores of requests for public appearances, and obligations to the Canadian skating community, all the while mastering a sharp learning curve on how to comport themselves as Olympic and world champions in all circumstances. They were trying to come to grips with the staggering depth and breadth of what their skating, and their titles, had meant to others. And they also wanted, and needed, to protect the privacy of their families.

They were constantly having to answer questions from both the media and the public about their relationship, replying with some variation of "skating and business partners; close friends for life; a special relationship but not romantically involved."

They had no previous template for that spring and summer. While charting their detailed skating plans for 2010–11, diligently training and building their competitive programs, they often had to convert to business or public speaking mode "with just a flick of the switch," as Tessa says.

And . . . they were exhausted.

The intense and injury-affected two years culminating in their Olympic triumph had taken a huge physical toll on them, and the post-Games whirlwind had obliterated any possibility of meaningful rest and recovery.

Soon they began declining most public engagements, staying in what Tessa calls "the

bubble of Canton" and embracing the familiarity of their primary loves: training and skating with each other and spending their days on the ice with other top-notch dancers, most notably Meryl Davis and Charlie White. The Olympics and Worlds had distanced the Canadians and Americans from the rest of the international field, and had inaugurated what would surely be a head-to-head battle for the next three-plus years.

While publicly they had committed only to the 2010–11 season, Tessa and Scott knew they were back for the full cycle. It made no practical sense to return for a single non-Olympic year.

Left: Tessa and Scott speaking in front of fans.
Below: (top) On the ice during a Roots photoshoot; *(bottom)* on the ice in Korea with skaters.

Above and opposite: A training session at the Arctic Edge rink in Canton, Michigan.

The music and basic choreography were chosen for their tango in the newly instituted short dance, and for their energetic, technically demanding "Hip Hip Chin Chin" Latin free dance.

They were in serious training, trying to evolve their athleticism and artistry to a higher level, but the pain in Tessa's legs returned "and then some." It was no longer restricted to the front of her shins, but was spreading to and concentrating in the back compartments of her calves, where it felt like it stabbed right into her bones.

Doctors at London's Fowler Kennedy Sport Medicine Clinic, who had performed her compartment syndrome operation in October 2008, suggested a more aggressive surgery this time. So, almost two years to the day after her first operation, the surgical team removed pieces of tissue from all the compartments in the fronts and backs of her lower legs.

In the recovery period that followed, Tessa experienced much more pain with every movement than she had in 2008.

Tessa and Scott knew just how daunting the road to recovery would be, but their earlier experience had armed them with a positive ally.

"We were so much better at communicating than we were in 2008," Tessa explains. "We were most proud of how we came back together back then."

The previous surgery had triggered the only real major problem they'd had in their relationship, as they'd become isolated from each other. That distance had

taken many months of work and frank discussion to close, and they weren't going to let it happen again. Scott, who desperately needed a rest anyway, came home to Ilderton and didn't skate for three weeks, keeping fit through off-ice training. They saw each other frequently during Tessa's painful rehabilitation, and were together at the Thompson Arena on the campus of the University of Western Ontario in November when she took her first few steps on the ice.

"Getting back together before was a long, hard road," Scott says. "And we didn't want to go back down that path. I'm still thankful for that opportunity to be supportive, although I wish it didn't have to be because Tess went under the knife again. It's pretty cliché, but every time you have a little breakdown like that — I mean we both care so much — when you start putting it back together it makes it stronger. All these problems we had along

through the free dance, pain in Tessa's quadriceps forced them to withdraw. So they would enter Worlds in Moscow with just that half-competition under their belts.

The world championships had been scheduled to begin in Tokyo on March 21, but the devastating Tohoku earthquake and tsunami postponed them until late April, with Moscow winning a bidding war against five other cities, including Vancouver, to replace Tokyo as host.

TESSA AND SCOTT WERE REALISTIC ABOUT THE Worlds because they hadn't been able to train diligently enough. And after four months of surgery recovery, the pain had returned to Tessa's legs every time they skated. But the Canadians still established a new benchmark for the nascent short

I'M STILL THANKFUL FOR THAT OPPORTUNITY TO BE SUPPORTIVE, ALTHOUGH I WISH IT DIDN'T HAVE TO BE BECAUSE TESS WENT UNDER THE KNIFE AGAIN . . . ALL THESE PROBLEMS WE HAD ALONG THE WAY HELPED US BUILD THE STRONG CONNECTIONS THAT WE HAD AT THE 2014 AND 2018 OLYMPICS." —Scott

the way helped us build the strong connections that we had at the 2014 and 2018 Olympics."

Recognizing that they'd returned to competition too early in 2008, they dropped out of the 2011 Nationals, and returned to Canton in December. They skated only twenty minutes a day for the first couple of weeks, then began to build up the time and the intensity, aiming for the Four Continents competition in Taipei in March.

Informed by their 2008–9 experiences, they consciously lowered their expectations. In the dance world, as they well knew, any suspicion that competitors were not fully fit or trained could severely affect perception, and therefore marks — particularly in the Program Components Score (PCS); a late-season return to competition was often politically perilous.

At Four Continents, they narrowly defeated Meryl and Charlie in the short dance, but partway

dance with 74.29 points to take a narrow lead over their training partners.

Meryl and Charlie skated strongly in the free dance to become the first dancers from the U.S. to win a world championship. Tessa and Scott took the silver. With American siblings Maia and Alex Shibutani moving up to the bronze, the top three teams in the world were all being coached by Marina Zoueva and Igor Shpilband.

"It was hard physically," Tessa recalls. "We had ambitious programs: our Latin free dance was quite challenging but we didn't have the mileage."

"We got beat," Scott says. "We were fine with the results. And we were happy for Meryl and Charlie. We knew the work that they put in, how consistent they were in training day after day."

As the season ended with exhibition tours through Asia and Canada, Tessa and Scott felt optimistic about the 2011–12 season — "Look out,

Above: Posing during the Finlandia Trophy in 2011. *Right:* On the podium during the 2011 World Figure Skating Championships in Moscow, Russia. From left, Tessa and Scott; their coaches Igor Shpilband and Marina Zoueva; Meryl Davis and Charlie White of USA; Maia Shibutani and Alex Shibutani of USA.

world," she said — because of the tribulations of 2010–11.

"The year might have been a write-off in some ways," Scott explains. "But it built a lot of the foundations as we headed into 2012, which arguably became even more successful than 2010. It was the way we had worked together. As much as it broke down in 2008 during the injury, it lifted up that year."

Enthused about the 2011–12 season, Scott, Tessa, and Marina chose George Gershwin music for their free dance and moved a segment of the previous year's undertrained free dance, "Hip Hip Chin Chin," into the short dance.

But during the spring and summer, when most of the heavy groundwork needed to be done for the competitive season, Tessa was still enduring serious leg pain. There were consultations in London about additional surgery, but she and Scott both disliked the idea of a third operation and recovery process in four years, especially when the net result so far hadn't been any long-term improvement. Perhaps more importantly, with more surgery there was the concern of excess scar tissue that could clog the leg compartments, exactly opposite of the intended result.

It was then that Bruce Craven, a noted sport physiotherapist and strength and conditioning coach from Saskatoon, came into their lives and began spending a lot of time in Canton.

"He was the first person to ask why the pain kept coming back, then concluded that it must be an issue with my mechanics," Tessa recalls. "How I was working, how I was using my muscles. The patterns my brain was using to activate my muscles."

Thus began a long, concentrated, and painful process of getting Tessa to retrain her body to take the load off her shins and calves and shift it to bigger muscles such as the hamstrings and glutes.

"It's kind of like learning to write with your other hand," she says. "I had seventeen or eighteen years of skating a certain way, of walking a certain way."

She had to alter completely the way she sat, the way she walked, the way she did squats and other gym exercises, her "loading" position to push her skate blade, the manner in which she stroked, her positions into lifts. Everything. To make it become second nature would require more than just a single season, so it was necessary for Craven to be a tough taskmaster.

"I remember Bruce following us down the hall and saying, 'Nope, you're walking wrong, you're not activating your glutes, you're not pushing off,'" she says, laughing about it now. "I didn't want to move because I knew I would be doing it wrong."

Scott joined the arduous sessions to support his partner — "It was so lovely of him," she says — but also because he's always been a technician and concluded that making such changes himself was going to make him, and the team, more powerful, with more efficient movements.

Along with overhauling their physiological technique, they built more cardio work, particularly interval training (energy bursts of varying lengths followed by rest), into their on-ice training, working on short segments of their program at a time.

Although there was still pain, Tessa eventually started to have some relief, even some pain-free days. And they could sense they were becoming stronger and faster skaters. An important side effect was that because this kind of physical restructuring

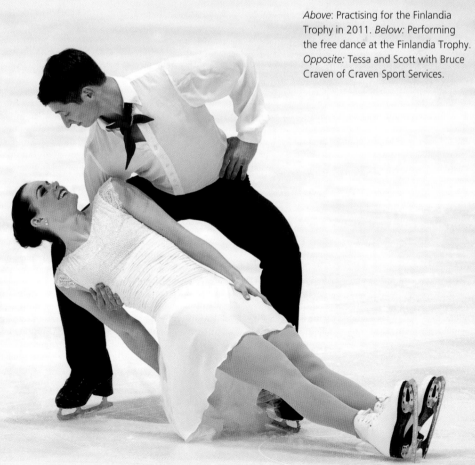

Above: Practising for the Finlandia Trophy in 2011. *Below:* Performing the free dance at the Finlandia Trophy. *Opposite:* Tessa and Scott with Bruce Craven of Craven Sport Services.

wasn't part of the Marina-Igor coaching process, Tessa and Scott had firmly taken the wheel of that part of their training.

"It was very much our project," Tessa says. "We had to take accountability, and grasp it."

Scott adds that he and his partner didn't want to continue through 2014 without being more evolved skaters than they had been in 2010.

"We knew we would have to be in order to beat Meryl and Charlie, but we also were ready to be students, and Bruce kind of brought this new dimension to our training that put us in the driver's seat," he explains. "*We* took control, *we* watched the video, *we* made the changes."

It was a significant departure from the way they'd physically prepared at Canton for eight years, and there were plateaus and setbacks, but even in the early part of the season, they could feel the positive effects.

They won their first competition, the Finlandia Trophy, and both events on the Grand Prix circuit: Skate Canada, ahead of compatriots

Kaitlyn Weaver and Andrew Poje, and Trophée Éric Bompard in Paris, over France's Nathalie Péchalat and Fabian Bourzat.

At the Grand Prix Final in Quebec City, Tessa and Scott lost again to Meryl and Charlie, mostly on the basis of a five-point deficit in the short dance. In media interviews afterward, in frustration, Scott questioned where his team's marks had gone, "especially the second mark."

"Which I still believe," he says now. "But if I were to do it again, I probably would have expressed myself differently."

That didn't help the tension between the top two dance couples in the world, which had already become noticeable at their training rink. As Tessa says, by then there wasn't a strong relationship left between the two once-close teams, but they still enjoyed, and were motivated by, training on the same ice with their talented American rivals.

By the time they reached February's Four Continents in Colorado Springs after winning Nationals, Tessa and Scott had adopted a more removed mental approach to the drama, politics, and judging foibles of the figure skating world around them. They employed a variety of catch phrases, like "screw it," to yank themselves back into their own space whenever they felt themselves straying, but essentially these were all synonyms for "we only care about what we can control ourselves."

They were confident, well trained, and "in the zone": "We were doing our own things in our own way, and it was powerful," Tessa explains.

"We're Canadian: we were daring them not to put us first," Scott says of the attitude they would try to maintain right through their final competitive performances, six years later.

They were having fun because for the first time in years Tessa's pain was manageable, sometimes even absent, and she was rebounding from it more quickly.

They finished second in the short dance, but won the free skate to beat Meryl and Charlie for the first time since the 2010 Worlds. The momentum continued into the world championships in Nice, France, as Tessa and Scott skated well and won both segments to handily defeat Meryl and Charlie for their second world title.

Above and opposite: On the ice at the Canadian National Exhibition in 2012.

But while their enormous competitive urges were satisfied, something else was not. They hadn't performed as well as they thought they could, so the win wasn't enough.

"In the kiss and cry I said, 'I'm sorry we didn't skate better,'" Tessa says. "We were in such a good place, but I realized it had now become more about the moment than just winning."

Scott says that in previous years they would have accepted that performance without question, but "now being trained and with the programs we were doing in training, it felt like the free dance came up a bit short. We were chasing that *feeling*, and it was probably the first time we realized that."

After Worlds, while Tessa and Scott performed on the Asian and Canadian Stars On Ice tours and took a little time off, there was a major shake-up back at the Arctic Edge Ice Arena in Canton. The Zoueva-Shpilband coaching partner-ship had split up; Igor had been dismissed. Marina would stay in Canton, while Igor would eventually begin coaching in Novi, Michigan.

"That was heartbreaking for us," Tessa said. "What we loved about Igor and Marina was their dynamic and how they complemented one another technically and artistically. The marriage of the talents. We didn't want them to split; we wanted to work with both of them."

Because Marina had played a much larger role in managing their skating, Tessa and Scott stayed in Canton, as did Meryl and Charlie and the Shibutani siblings, while Madison Chock and Evan Bates chose to go with Igor.

"We were closer to Marina at the time," Scott says, but adds, "I'm pretty confident in saying that, knowing what we know now, we might have made a different decision."

Left: Tessa and Scott perform their polka short dance at the 2013 Worlds Competition. *Right:* Performing at the Canadian National Exhibition in 2012.

WITH IGOR DEPARTED, THE HIGH-stakes rivalry between Tessa and Scott and Meryl and Charlie intensifying, and both teams maturing into their mid-twenties, the dynamics at the training centre were changing. Tessa and Scott credit Marina with making sure that, as before, a second coach was with them at competitions when she was with another couple. Johnny Johns was particularly helpful.

And while they may not have seized "that feeling" in their Worlds free dance, they had been buoyed by reclaiming their world title. That contributed heavily to what, in retrospect, was a major mistake. They didn't see physiotherapist Bruce Craven as often, and backslid from the interval training and some of the other energy- and muscle-preserving techniques he had so rigorously drilled into them.

"We got a little casual with it," Scott concedes. "We didn't pay the price in October, November, and December; we paid the price in February at Four Continents."

The 2013 Worlds, which they assumed would be their last, were scheduled for March in London, their hometown, which added an exciting spark to the entire season.

For their polka short dance they chose "And the Waltz Goes On," which had been composed by actor Anthony Hopkins when he was just starting his career. Hoping to express their evolving artistic innovation and maturity, they went with *Carmen* for the free dance. They brought in Jennifer Swan, whom Tessa had known since she was six when Jennifer was her first dance teacher in London, to work with Marina on *Carmen*.

"It was fun, we felt we were really expressing ourselves," Tessa says. "Here's music people had used a million times; so how do we make it different?"

By being truer to the original, simple story-line than most skaters ever had, Scott explains. The male character, impassioned by Carmen's sexuality, becomes obsessed and controlling while she plays him. It was to be edgy and provocative, "making people feel slightly uncomfortable," Tessa says.

The main goal for 2012–13 was to show-case their versatility and highlight a different side of Virtue and Moir, "maybe out there a bit," so that they could return to their perceived

Above and opposite: Dancing the *Carmen* routine at the 2012–13 Grand Prix Final in Sochi.

strengths for the Sochi Olympic year. It was also meant to offer a stylistic contrast to Meryl and Charlie.

"Maybe this is more in hindsight, but when we went out in 2013 and did this program we really loved, we found that that kind of edgy artistry was more of a strength than the lyrical approach that we had in 2010 and would have in 2014," Scott says.

Although they didn't find it offensive in any way, judges and officials advised Tessa and Scott to tone down the provocative program to make it more widely acceptable. They made the adjustments, but now wish they'd stayed with the original.

They loved *Carmen*, stripping their skating down so that every single moment counted, which they viewed as a huge step forward artistically and technically. But they were always concerned that it was, as Scott describes it, "a three-and-a-half-minute program." It lacked punch in the final thirty seconds, but they were unsuccessful in convinc-

ing Marina to ratchet it up to a more memorable climax.

They won both Skate Canada and the Rostelecom Cup in Moscow before facing Meryl and Charlie at the Grand Prix Final, which was the test event for the Sochi Olympic venue.

The Americans won both segments, with Tessa and Scott performing what they admitted was a substandard final lift in the free dance.

After claiming their fifth National title in January, Tessa and Scott headed to Four Continents in Osaka, where they finished first in the short dance. But two minutes into the free dance, Tessa could not go on because of severe cramping in her legs. They were given a three-minute break to recover — a rule which was later changed when too many teams began taking advantage of it — and returned, but finished second behind Meryl and Charlie's performance to selections from *Notre-Dame de Paris*.

Tessa, the ultra-competitive athlete, felt she had let her partner, coaches, and entire support team down, and still wonders whether she could have pushed through the pain. But Scott constantly reminds her that she had already prevailed over severe pain to even reach that point of the season, and that program. He calls it foolish that for the first half of the season they hadn't heeded the training lessons they'd learned the year before.

At Worlds, before an adoring hometown crowd in London, they didn't skate well in the short dance, but rebounded to unleash a beautiful, provocative free dance. Meryl and Charlie still won both segments to reclaim the world title.

"We got a standing ovation in our hometown, which was great, and we thought we won the free dance, but it was too late," Scott recalls. "Plus, perception is reality. Because we had stopped in Four Continents, any little weakness becomes a matter of 'They must not be trained.'"

They were heading into their second Olympic season feeling that things had been turning against them in some way, to the point that Tessa was seriously contemplating whether she should even return for one last competitive season.

But in May she and Scott attended the Canadian Olympic camp in Vancouver, and,

inspired by the displays of banners and the five rings, and memories of 2010, she realized how much the Games feeling had meant to her personally. Empowered, she knew she and her partner would do whatever it took to get through, and enjoy, the Olympic season.

Below: On the ice at the Sochi Grand Prix Final.
Opposite: Tessa and Scott receive a standing ovation at the 2013 Worlds in their hometown of London, Ontario.

WITH THE LENGTHENING STRING OF losses to Meryl and Charlie, the approaching, crushing pressure of the Sochi Games, and the changes in both the coaching structure and their relationship with Meryl and Charlie, Tessa says the training atmosphere at Canton felt "a little toxic." She and Scott were feeling increasingly isolated there.

That sense was compounded by an uncharacteristically late choice of free dance music. Normally Marina would have a number of ideas for them in the early spring, but they say she didn't really have one in 2013, and those that Scott and Tessa brought to her were met with a lukewarm reception. Tessa and Scott had a reference point: something that made them feel like they did when they listened to "Somewhere in Time," which Marie-France Dubreuil and Patrice Lauzon had skated to in 2008. But they couldn't find it.

"And it got to the point where we had to do something," Tessa said. She, Scott, and Marina finally agreed upon two pieces by Russian composer Alexander Glazunov — "The Seasons," and a waltz — plus an ending piano concerto by Alexander Scriabin, from the same turn-of-the-century era.

Normally, they'd aim for clean run-throughs by Canada Day, but didn't even settle upon the music until June, and hadn't even begun choreographing it. They thought they could find a story to tell in it, but weren't quite sure what it was.

The music delay, pressure, and sense of aloneness set the training season off on the wrong foot, and the negative energy caused some arguments and tension between the lifelong friends.

This was the summer and autumn in which a crew from Canada's W Network spent sixty-five days with them filming the *Tessa and Scott* documentary series; the seven-installment series would

"NO MATTER WHAT WAS GOING TO HAPPEN, WE WERE GOING TO GO AND DARE THEM TO PUT US SECOND, AND GIVE THEM EVERYTHING WE HAD."—*Scott*

Above: Relaxing at the cottage with Mike Babcock; *Opposite (top):* Tessa and Scott promote their W Network reality show; *(bottom)* showing off their silver medals at the Sochi Olympics.

begin airing in January 2014 in thirteen countries. Such a major project in the short Olympic season was a gamble, they knew, but they felt that since they were not on social media, it would help people get to know them better, and Marina agreed that they should accept it. Tessa and Scott became close to the crew, which helped insulate them from what they viewed as a negative training atmosphere in Canton.

B Y DECEMBER THEY'D COME TOGETHER TIGHTLY again, resolving to make Sochi their experience and no one else's. The "screw it" mentality.

They won Skate Canada and Trophée Éric Bompard, and in the Grand Prix Final set a world record score of 190.0, which Meryl and Charlie surpassed a few minutes later with 191.35. Scott says that, looking at the elements, they deserved to finish second.

They loved their "Cheek to Cheek" short program but were still struggling to find the storyline for the free dance, which was supposed to represent the arc of their relationship, picking up where 2010's Mahler had left off. But it was too confusing for an audience to relate to.

It was after the Grand Prix Final that Tessa and Scott emphatically recommitted to the "screw

it" philosophy and to making Sochi their own experience.

"No matter what was going to happen, we were going to go and dare them to put us second, and give them everything we had," Scott says. "In many ways that was an important season for us because while maybe it wasn't our best work, program-wise, we did it all ourselves. We worked hard at it: Even 'Seasons' at some point had a little sparkle. It might not have had that extra drive to win an Olympics against a team the calibre of Meryl and Charlie, but it had something."

Just before the Games, the French newspaper *L'Équipe* reported that American and Russian judges had made a deal to help Russia win the brand-new team event, and Meryl and Charlie the individual ice dance gold medal. The Code of Points scoring system contained some checks and balances against deal-making, but at the highest level, a few slivers of points could make the difference between gold and silver medals. Additionally, over time, a whispering campaign could potentially be waged to influence "group think."

The story ripped through the skating world and Canadian Olympic community in Sochi, but Tessa and Scott were mostly unfazed. They had long ago placed their general trust in the revamped judging system, and, more critically, they had learned that it was imperative to keep all outside forces outside their Olympic bubble, to maintain the focus and clarity they needed to compete as fiercely as they could. It was much harder on their parents, who had already concluded that their children were entering a battle that they could not win.

What did bother Tessa and Scott was that Marina marched with the American team in the opening ceremonies, further increasing their feelings of isolation. Almost as if noticing that, Canadian hockey coach Mike Babcock visited them in the athletes' village gym and cafeteria, advising them to be strong "between the ears." And long-time mentor Patrice Lauzon, coaching another team, came to every one of their practices and even visited them in the warm-up area right before the individual free dance, wordlessly touching Tessa's face in a gesture of support.

In the short dance and free dance of both the team and individual events, Meryl and Charlie finished first and Tessa and Scott second, by significant margins. The Canadians took two silver medals and the Americans their own gold and a bronze for the team event. But Tessa and Scott felt

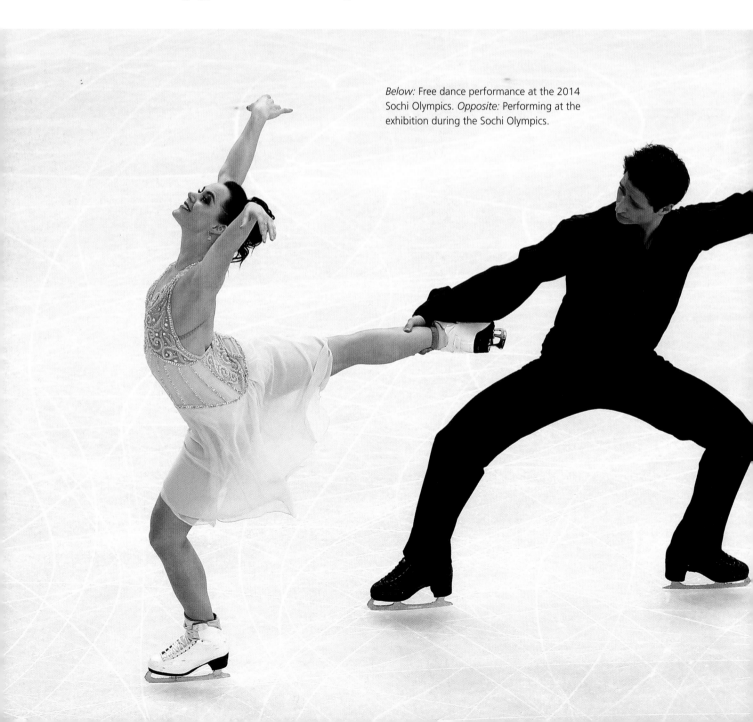

Below: Free dance performance at the 2014 Sochi Olympics. *Opposite:* Performing at the exhibition during the Sochi Olympics.

they had skated well in three of the four segments, although they'd had to work hard for every mark in the team event.

Back in Canada, Paul MacIntosh, who had coached them so long ago, was angered by the judging in the individual portion. "Those two days Scott and Tessa were better than the other team," he fumed. "Maybe not all season, and maybe not for two seasons, but those two days they were."

But Tessa says that, given the circumstances, they really were content with what they'd done. And, inspired by freestyle skier Jenn Heil, who was

second in Vancouver after finishing first in Turin four years earlier, they chose to view it as winning the silver rather than losing the gold.

That attitude, both families have since said, made their parents very proud.

Shortly afterward, Scott was open with the Olympic media about the concerns they'd had that season with Marina.

"I think we were just searching for answers, and I really hope that was never perceived as whining or being ungrateful, because we weren't," he says.

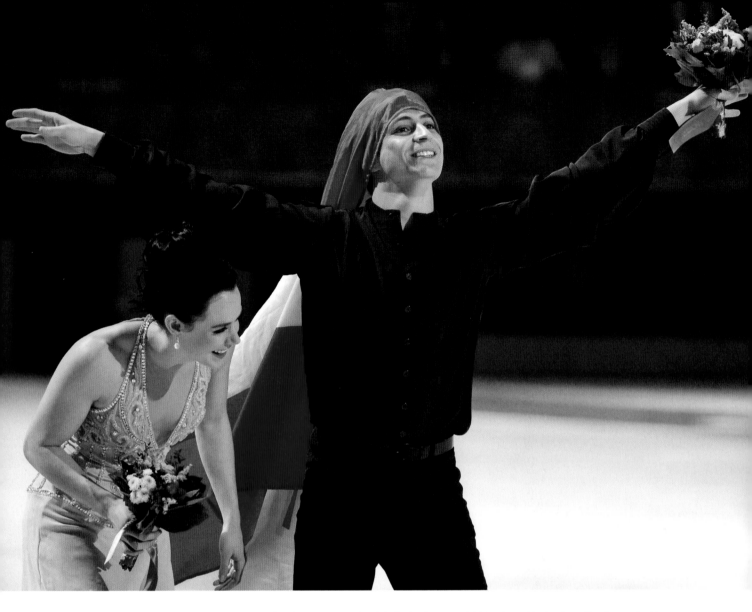

Above: Celebrating on the ice at the 2014 Sochi Olympics. *Opposite: (clockwise from top left):* Posing with the Canadian flag at Sochi; Tessa with the Sochi flame; Scott and Patrick Chan *(right)* cheer on the Canadian Women's hockey team.

"We don't have any shame finishing second: there's part of us that are fans of Meryl and Charlie too. Their style isn't the same as ours, but we see them train; we know that they do their work every day and that they're consistent, very consistent. They were together a long time. In one Olympics, we were on top, and as much as you want to stand on the top spot, as athletes we have respect for other athletes who do."

In the kiss and cry, Tessa and Scott knew they were about to take a major break from competition.

"I thought we were done," she says.

Fulfilling their promise to make Sochi their own experience, they had already enjoyed the athletes' village, the buses, and the bike rides to the cafeteria more than they ever had, and after com-peting they fully immersed themselves in the rest of the Games.

"That part of the Olympic experience was our best one, not Vancouver, not Pyeongchang," Scott smiles. "Which is hilarious because when people think of our Olympic story, they're afraid to mention Sochi."

They were slightly apprehensive about the return home, wondering if Canadians might feel they'd let the country down, but they found exactly the opposite reaction.

"It was an outpouring of support," Tessa recalls. "It was crazy, it was soooo nice."

But Canton, their home for eleven years, was home no more, and it was time to move on to the next part of their lives.

"THAT MOMENT YOU HAVE ON THE ICE TOGETHER, BEFORE YOU GET FEEDBACK FROM THE JUDGES AND COACHES, BEFORE YOU HEAR FROM THE FANS, IS ALWAYS THE MOST IMPORTANT TO US . . . WE WOULD HAVE STAYED OUT THERE FOREVER IF WE COULD." —*Scott*

Tessa and Scott celebrate their Olympic gold medal win in Pyeongchang.

Chapter Seven

GOLD AGAIN

"WE OPENED THE DOOR, TO SHARE OURSELVES
WITH THE REST OF THE WORLD."—*Scott*

LTHOUGH THEY'D INDICATED THEY WERE taking time off, Tessa and Scott never really made a formal announcement that they were not going to compete any more.

"We're fans of announcing when you really do have news," Scott says. "Like you're going to come back."

For both of them 2014 and 2015 flew by in a virtual blur, especially their first season without "amateur" competition in more than two decades.

"It was what we called 'the year of saying yes,'" Tessa laughs. "Before, we really had to say no to everything. It was fun to all of a sudden have some freedom to say 'yes' to charity events, business ventures, a lot of different things."

Scott moved back to Ilderton and Tessa to London, but they were seldom there for more than a few days at a time. They performed in Stars on Ice and other exhibition skating, and accepted numerous speaking engagements, usually as a team because "as much time as we'd spent together, we loved working together more," Scott says. They emphasized, especially to younger audiences, that their silver medal in Sochi was as important to them as their Vancouver gold. They also started a fundraising golf tournament to raise money for the Thames Valley Children's Centre and to give back to the Ilderton Skating Club, which had launched

their careers, and Scott would occasionally work with young skaters on the Ilderton ice.

Scott, fulfilling a long-ago promise to his mother, Alma, finished his high-school degree by distance learning, while Tessa, who'd been working toward a psychology degree at the University of Windsor, took three courses in one semester on campus at the University of Western Ontario near her home, which was difficult with their heavy travel schedule. They both chuckle at being a decade older than most of their peers.

Tessa had switched her educational target from a law degree to an MBA and was taking a deeper interest in their sponsors' companies, beyond simple endorsements. She wanted to understand their internal workings: corporate structure, market implementation, national and international objectives, workplace dynamics. Her most consuming and fulfilling project was with Canadian jewellery retailer Hillberg and Berk, for which she designed and helped package about a hundred pieces in the Tessa Virtue Collection.

Scott, meanwhile, purchased and renovated a house near Ilderton with his brother Charlie, who, he concedes, had to do most of the work because of Scott's travel commitments.

They were far removed from the skating world in which they'd been immersed for so long, but did pay attention to the international scene because they were going to do some on-air commentary for TSN and work the 2016 Worlds for CBC-TV.

In the absence of Tessa and Scott, Meryl and Charlie, and a couple of other retired teams, a new young couple had ascended spectacularly to the top of international ice dancing.

After finishing thirteenth at the 2014 Worlds, Gabriella Papadakis and Guillaume Cizeron — with Romain Haguenauer, one of their coaches — had relocated from their native France to Montreal. They were training under the Canadian husband-and-wife coaching team of Marie-France Dubreuil and Patrice Lauzon, who as competitors had won two world championship silver medals. In their first season under Marie-France and Patrice, they won the world championship in Shanghai, at

> "THERE'S SOMETHING TO BE LEARNED FROM PERFORMING ON DEMAND . . . IN COMPETITION, YOU'RE HYPERSENSITIVE TO HOW YOU FEEL, AND EVERY DETAIL HAS TO BE RIGHT. BUT WE LEARNED THAT SOMETIMES YOU HAVE TO PUT THE FEELING ASIDE AND DO IT." —*Tessa*

the ages of nineteen and twenty, reminiscent of Tessa and Scott's youthful triumphs. Americans Madison Chock and Evan Bates were second, and Canadians Kaitlyn Weaver and Andrew Poje took the bronze after winning silver the year before.

After Gabriella's concussion kept them out of competition for the first half of the season, Papadakis and Cizeron would dominate the field to win a second World title in 2016, with Tessa and Scott providing commentary for the Canadian TV audience.

Meanwhile, Scott and Tessa were doing a number of exhibitions, training their programs for a week, only a few minutes a day, at the rinks in Ilderton and nearby Exeter before heading out to perform. And they were gathering certain coping skills they couldn't get from competitive skating.

"There's something to be learned from performing on demand," Tessa says. "For instance, we did thirty-six shows at the CNE in eighteen days. You just have to make it happen no matter what. In competition, you're hypersensitive to how you feel, and every detail has to be right. But we learned that sometimes you have to put the feeling aside and do it."

Their show programs were being choreographed and coached by a variety of professionals, including Jeffrey Buttle, Marie-France and Patrice, and off-ice dancer Sam Chouinard, causing an idea to percolate.

"I think it started sinking into the back of our minds that not everybody does things the way we'd been doing things the last ten years," Scott says. "Maybe we *do* have some unfinished business in skating.'"

They had been nibbling around the edges of a return to competition, subtly trying to reach into each other's brains, to figure out what the other thought of the idea. Task-oriented Tessa was unsatisfied by show skating and by her schedule, which was always full but not directed toward a single goal. She felt she wasn't doing any one thing well enough. During Stars on Ice tours Scott had spent a lot of time picking Patrice Lauzon's brain about every aspect of life, and in one meeting he wondered aloud what it might look like if he and Tessa were to train at Patrice and Marie-France's school in Montreal.

"And Patch [Patrice Lauzon] said, 'Oh, I think Tessa wants to do it, I just don't know if you have it in you.'"

That startling answer shocked Scott, making him realize just how badly he did want to return. In July 2015, he and Tessa flew to Beijing and skated in a show for just a few minutes, and before boarding a late return flight the next day, they took a trip to the Great Wall of China. During the two-hour drive, they had a what-if discussion: where would they train if they returned, who would coach them, what would be their philosophical approach? And it became

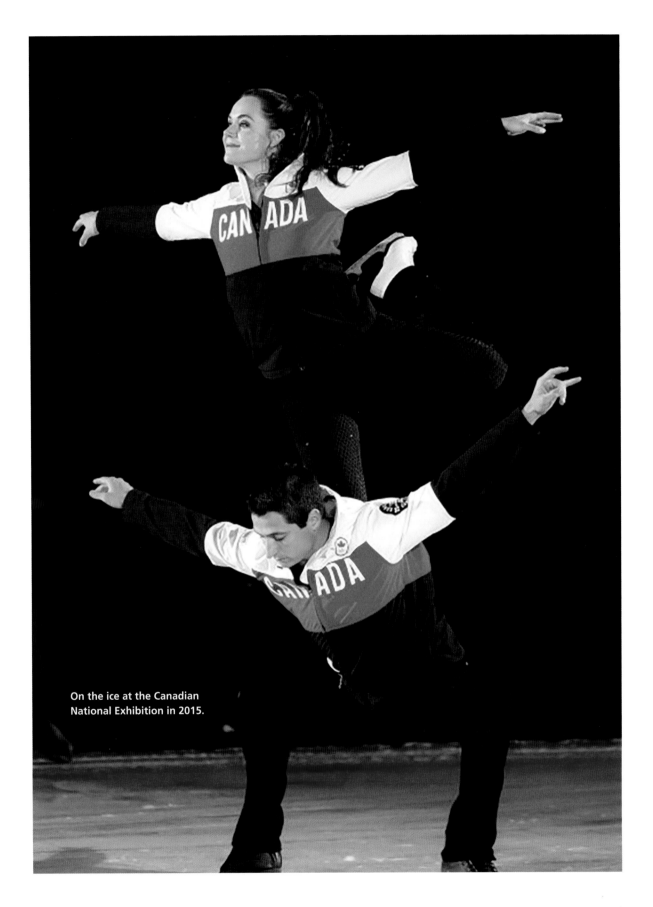

On the ice at the Canadian
National Exhibition in 2015.

obvious that they were on the same track toward a decision one couldn't possibly make without the other's full commitment: they wanted to come back.

"That was the final confluence," Tessa says.

But Patrice and Marie-France didn't accept Scott and Tessa right away. There was a phone interview with tough, very pointed questions — among them, what their goals were and how they would react if those goals weren't accomplished. The skaters wondered if the coaches felt they might have scared them off, but to Tessa and Scott, it was an impressive communicative beginning. Marie-France and Patrice were their friends, and idols, and wanted to make sure Tessa and Scott were returning for the right reasons. Wanting to advance ice dancing technically and artistically and to push against the boundaries of their sport, they knew they had to work with Marie-France and Patrice, or no one.

Above and opposite: Tessa and Scott lace up at Gadbois in 2016. *Opposite: (bottom)* Walking the Great Wall of China in 2015.

"If they had said no . . . " Tessa begins, and Scott finishes: "that would have been the end of it."

But the coaches said yes, and in December 2015 they started working secretly together while assembling a show program with Marie-France and choreographer David Wilson.

By January they were at the Gadbois Centre in southwest Montreal. They recognized the irony of returning to a similar situation they had left in Canton — training with the other top team in the world and working with the same coaches — but relished the finest part of what they'd always had with Meryl and Charlie: being pushed and inspired by the best, every day. And Gabriella Papadakis and Guillaume Ceziron were very welcoming. "The whole school was; they had created a special culture — inspiring, motivating, and friendly — and that stems from Marie and Patch," Tessa says.

TESSA AND SCOTT WERE TRAINING FOR SHOW programs, at a different energy level than that required to defend a world title, so they stayed out of Gabriella's and Guillaume's way. But they were also working diligently on the Midnight Blues, the compulsory rhythm of the 2016–17 short dance, and skating people were starting to whisper about their return.

So they decided to announce their return on CBC on Saturday, February 20 — two years, to the day, from the free dance in Pyeongchang — because now they did have real news. Not wanting to overshadow the competitors at Worlds, they felt the announcement was far enough in advance for the buzz to subside by the time they got behind their microphones.

With Gabriella having recovered from a pre-season concussion, she and Guillaume swept to the world title in Boston, exciting Tessa and Scott, who wanted to train with, and compete against, the best. They began turning down outside engagements to train more, and worked extra practice hours during the Stars on Ice spring tours.

On June 6, they began formal training in Montreal for the 2017 Worlds in Helsinki, and the 2018 Olympics in Pyeongchang.

Above: Performing at Ice Legends in Geneva, Switzerland, in April 2016.
Opposite: Rehearsing for Stars on Ice in May 2016.

and museums just up the hill, and a bustling downtown core a few minutes further out. Too far away from southwestern Ontario for frequent hometown trips, "we moved our whole lives there, and I think that did have an impact on us," Scott says.

The two years of outside perspective they had gained had made them different people and skating students; so did working with coaches who Tessa and Scott felt fostered a strong sense of working on a plan together with them.

And they all had a plan for major change.

Reviewing tapes of 2014, Tessa and Scott had concluded that much could be improved upon, and Patrice agreed.

After years informed by Russian style, they would ease toward a more traditional British carriage, while still maintaining the stylistic elements that had always made them "Tessa and Scott." But the much bigger adjustment would come in their stroking style: the glide of the blades, the knee action, placement of the hip on circles, and other functional details. So, as they had done four years earlier with Bruce Craven reshaping their mechanics, they started to tear apart some basic skating habits in order to rebuild them. Scott and Tessa had always been taught to use a relatively harsh, quick stride to get into beautiful positions. But what Patrice envisioned was to meld that with an ease of motion, a more effortless use of the blade in working with the ice to eliminate friction and generate more speed.

"We loved the idea, and were excited to work tirelessly at it," Scott said of the new blueprint. "Trying to do that after an eighteen-year career was a daunting task. But we knew that our goal for 2018 was that we had to look so different. Nobody wanted to see us the way we were in 2010 and 2014. Even if we accomplished just 40 percent of those changes, that would be worth it."

From the experience of altering their biomechanics in 2012–14, they knew it would likely be the second season before significant results really began to show. Rejuvenated by the new process, they embraced the rigorous work and the technical team stroking sessions, although through the early summer Scott would lie exhausted on his couch most of the weekend just to regather energy for the following week.

S COTT AND TESSA MOVED INTO APARTMENTS IN the vibrant area near the Atwater Market in Montreal, close to the training arena, where they could bike the trails along the Lachine Canal. The distinct urban Montreal culture and energy level was a stark change from Canton, with three of the country's top restaurants in the immediate vicinity, art galleries

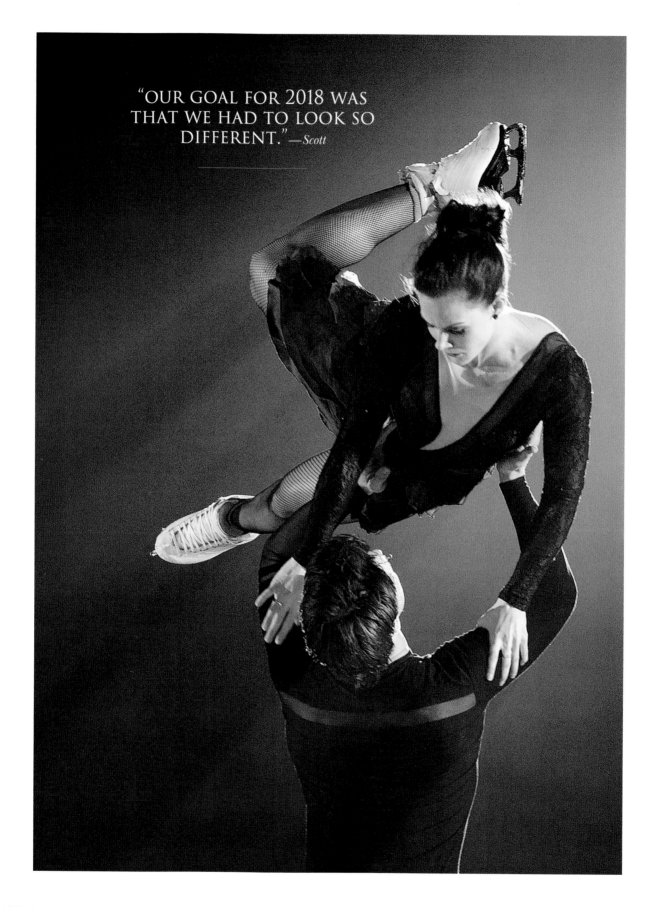

"OUR GOAL FOR 2018 WAS
THAT WE HAD TO LOOK SO
DIFFERENT." —*Scott*

Above: (top) In Pyeongchang with Dave Campbell; *(middle):* with J.-F. Ménard *(left)* and John Flood *(right)*; *(bottom):* With Scotty Livingston and fellow trainees. *Opposite:* Ice Legends, 2016.

But they loved the atmosphere and their compact neighbourhood, which, coincidentally, housed the training gym used by B2ten, the private sector consortium founded by Jenn Heil and her husband, Dominick Gauthier, to provide fund-

ing and sport-related resources for elite Canadian athletes. B2ten had paid for Tessa's physiotherapist Mary Brannagan to be in Vancouver in 2010, and the organization came back into their life in Montreal. Through the Pyeongchang Games and beyond, Tessa and Scott would publicly emphasize that they could not have returned the way they did, financially or psychologically, without B2ten's massive help.

"We really had to prove ourselves, that we were ready for them," Tessa says of the initial B2ten stages. "Eager to do our sport in a different way and accept their knowledge, advice, and insight."

They had to run their training as a business, with monthly board meetings of up to fifteen people: the main coach, Patrice, at the centre, with Marie-France, Tessa, and Scott, joined by B2ten mental preparation coach Jean-François Ménard, physiologist Chris Rozdilsky, strength and conditioning coaches Jaime Livingston and Scotty Livingston, physiotherapist John Flood, osteopath Dave Campbell, Pilates instructor Ann McMillan, nutritionist Alexia de Macar, naturopath Kim McQueen, and massage therapist Kimberly Wong.

It was an integrated team effort managed by Dominick Gauthier with frequent, sometimes daily, communication about the skaters' progress. They were working out with elite Canadian athletes such as Erik Guay, Mikael Kingsbury, and Alex Bilodeau, and physiologist Chris Rozdilsky was gathering data that would prove enormously helpful, especially in the Olympic year. They wore special shirts all day and night for two weeks at a time to monitor their breathing and sleeping patterns and energy input and output. Eventually — and especially after a big energy depletion heading into the 2017 Worlds — it was determined that, as a team, Tessa and Scott needed a 3:1 ratio of work to rest in a week. It became a matter of spreading their available energy over a whole week, and competition weeks were different from training or off weeks. Every detail was analyzed, right down to how their meal preparation or pre-bed routine time affected them.

It was a scientific approach to energy management in a sport that Scott says lags far behind

Above: Working on their routines at Gadbois, 2016. *Opposite: (left)* Performing to Prince at the 2017 Canadian Tire National Skating Championships in Ottawa, Canada; *(right)* performing to "Latch" at the 2016 Grand Prix Final in Marseille, France.

most Olympic sports in physiological analysis: "We're old school in skating. The theme is always: the more hours the better." That theme had led to overtraining, contributing considerably to the serious leg issues that had afflicted Tessa for the better part of six years.

Tessa and Scott felt close to the entire group, and considered them an integral part of their journey throughout the next two years.

To heighten the sudden impact they wanted to make in their return to competition, Marie-France designed a short dance from three pieces by the iconic artist Prince. Incorporating blues and hip-hop, it allowed Tessa and Scott to highlight the elevated performance skills they had developed in show skating, while emphasizing enhanced

technical skills. The free dance, which they'd choreographed back in February, opened with "Pilgrims on a Long Journey," a beautiful piece from the video game Child of Light, and revolved around "Latch," a song by British electronic music duo Disclosure, featuring vocals by Sam Smith. It was the first time in the competitive skating setting that Tessa and Scott had gone totally contemporary.

Tessa and Scott like to point out that what the public perceived as their storybook comeback was not at all a smooth arc. There were many setbacks and detours, especially in the early part of the 2016–17 season. They were rebuilding their skating, adjusting to a new coaching team and philosophy, and discovering that competing as twenty-seven- and twenty-nine-year-olds presented a different dynamic than before they left for two years. They also sensed that some members of the skating community, even former supporters in Canada, believed they shouldn't have returned because they'd already accomplished everything; moreover, the sport had changed, and Scott and Tessa might not be able to keep up.

In their first competition in Montreal, that summer, they were tired and didn't perform well. On the spot, they summoned performance psychologist J.-F. Ménard to the dressing room. Patrice, Scott recalls, was a little shocked at their intensity, and reminded them that it was their first competition in two years.

At their first Grand Prix event, Skate Canada in Mississauga, they narrowly beat Americans Madison Chock and Evan Bates, and actually lost the free dance. They had an immediate, and

harshly self-critical, debriefing with Marie-France and Patrice during which they now concede they were "maybe a little unrealistic." Their deeply rooted competitive urges had taken over, in stark contrast to their mood during the long spring and summer of training that had been centred on their own skating, on doing different things, and on bettering themselves. In essence, it was coaches and skaters learning more about each other under different circumstances.

Because they knew all the officials, volunteers, and many of the fans, there had been undue pressure at Skate Canada, and Tessa and Scott were glad to head to NHK in Japan and their first competition against Gabriella and Guillaume. On the way, however, Scott visited a lifelong friend who had fallen gravely ill. It left him shaken and emotionally drained. For both him and his partner,

Above: Tessa and Scott off-ice during a practice session for the 2017 Canadian Tire National Skating Championships. *Opposite: (above)* Tessa and Scott at the 2016 NHK Trophy in Sapporo, Japan; *(below)* at the 2017 Worlds in Helsinki, Finland.

*"*I JUST LEANED ON TESSA,
AND SHE WAS SO STRONG
. . . THE ONLY TIME
I FELT COMFORTABLE
WAS WHEN I HAD
HER HAND IN MINE,
AND WAS LOOKING
IN HER EYES.*"—Scott*

skating seemed a bit irrelevant in the face of such shattering reality, and NHK became a blur. Scott barely remembers beating the French team and setting a new short dance record in winning the competition.

"I just leaned on Tessa, and she was so strong," he says. "I think that really altered the dynamic of our partnership, again. Maybe she'd had to lean on me a little bit a couple of times when she was injured, but I totally relied on her then. The only time I felt comfortable was when I had her hand in mine, and was looking in her eyes."

Scott's best friend died while they were competing at NHK, and he flew home to speak at the funeral. It was a challenging time for Scott, and for the rest of the season he never recovered emotionally. Still, they won the Grand Prix Final for the first time, extending their own world short dance points record, then skated brilliantly to win their seventh

Canadian championship. Through NHK, the Grand Prix Final, and Nationals, Scott says, it was all about survival, drawing on their deep well of competitive history. Having to concentrate upon one element at a time had forced them to maintain a sharp focus, helping them skate up to their training expectations in three straight competitions.

Scott, trying to deal for the first time with the death of someone close, was still fighting physical and psychological fatigue through their victory at Four Continents, where their performance level fell off from the previous three events.

That spring Alma and Carol Moir's father, "Grampa Mac," who'd always been a huge influence on Scott and was his barometer of a life well lived, became ill. As he and Tessa headed to the world championships in Helsinki, Scott recalls, "I was in shock and numb and in survival mode." Tessa, who was also feeling the emotional pain, had never seen him so depleted.

They skated superbly in the short program, besting Gabriella and Guillaume by more than five points, but Scott had nothing left for the free dance. Two minutes in, he stumbled and one of his hands touched the ice. As he recovered, Tessa cracked, "Well, that was dramatic!" They continued, finishing second in the free dance to their French training partners, but beating them with a new world total-score record of 198.62 points.

In the kiss and cry, despite winning their third world championship to complete the first undefeated season of their career, an exhausted Scott was subdued, and embarrassed about his

Above and right: Scott with his Grampa Mac.
Opposite: (above) Performing at the 2016–17 Grand Prix Final in Marseille, France; *(below)* Scott during training at Gadbois in 2017.

fall; it meant that they didn't have the championship skate they had wanted to deliver. But with the help of mental prep coach J.-F. Ménard, he would come to realize "It was maybe exactly the motivation I needed: Would we have skated the same way we did in Pyeongchang if that didn't happen the year before? I would argue maybe not."

After Worlds, Scott had some important, uplifting final visits with Grampa Mac. And on April 21, Irven "Mac" MacCormack died, in his own home and surrounded by family.

Scott "disappeared" with close friends to the Muskoka region north of Toronto for several days in late April to rest, and to help himself deal with the deaths of his lifelong friend and his grandfather. He started to regain traction, and it was time for him and Tessa to begin their third, and final, Olympic season.

THE ICE DANCING FIELD FOR THE 2017–18 Olympic season would be deep. It comprised three different world champions (Tessa and Scott with three titles, Gabriella Papadakis and Guillaume Cizeron with two, and Italy's Anna Cappellini and Luca Lanotte, who had won Worlds in 2014). Seven different teams had won a total of eighteen world medals, but the overwhelming expectation was that, as in 2014, the Olympics were going to come down to a two-team race between couples training at the same rink under the same coaches.

All photos: **Practising for the Autumn Classic International in Pierrefonds, Quebec, 2017.**

In the spring, Tessa and Scott had a pivotal meeting with their coaches, similar in part to the one with Marina Zoueva in 2013. They had some concerns about the way in which a couple of things had been handled in Helsinki, and also wanted to make sure that their coaches felt they could win the Olympics, which Patrice and Marie-France did. The difference between that meeting and the one four years earlier in Canton, Scott says, was that Patrice really listened, and he took notes. He said he hadn't realized some things were problems, explained why they'd occurred, and then asked what Tessa and Scott needed from him and Marie-France going forward. But that spring Marie-France and Patrice also suggested things Tessa and Scott could do to help the coach–skater communication. And, more tellingly, that they needed to know that the skaters valued and needed them. It was a very evolved, adult set of discussions, and Tessa and Scott, who had toiled so conscientiously for so long on their own relationship, recognized the same forces at play between coaches and skaters: communicating and working to improve the team. After a year of learning about each other, they were getting a strong sense of the back-and-forth process, and understanding the strong essence they had as coaches and skaters.

"It was important because it starts how the rest of the year works out," Scott explains. "Which was that when we asked for something or challenged them, they did everything they could to answer that call, to build themselves as coaches. And they expected us to do the same as athletes."

Tessa adds: "It was also about understanding that their way of showing love or care was, in one case, this, and in another case, that. You really have to learn how another person works, and we'd done so much of that with each other."

They had become comfortable giving input to their coaches, and also about how Marie-France and Patrice would respond.

It was Marie-France who came up with the idea for the Latin short program using music by three iconic bands: the Rolling Stones' stirring "Sympathy for the Devil" as a samba, a cover version of the Eagles' "Hotel California" for the cruel duke. The story encompasses her struggle to fully know herself, and then to free herself. But it also involved her evolving relationship with the smitten writer whom she can at first manipulate, just as she's being played like a puppet by the men who control her. The concluding narrative had imprinted itself on popular culture: the writer and courtesan do fall deeply in love, but, in the end, she contracts tuberculosis and dies.

Above and right: Performing the *Moulin Rouge!* routine at the 2017 Autumn Classic International in Pierrefonds, Quebec. *Opposite: (above)* A crucial part of Tessa's pre-warm-up routine was to consult her "J.-F. notebook"; *(below)* Marie-France and Scott skate together during a practice session.

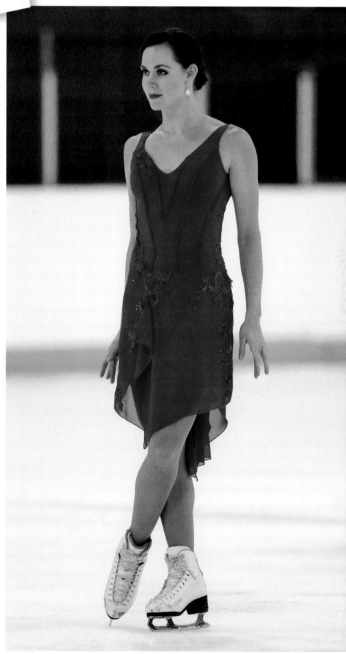

rhumba, and Santana's "Oye Como Va" for the cha-cha. They would have preferred the Eagles' version of "Hotel California" from the *Hell Freezes Over* album, but there was too much crowd noise. The Santana segment was meant to highlight the elements in the closing portion of the program.

"I wish people got to see what I got to see during the creative process," Scott marvels. "Watching the first part of that coming together, it was nothing short of genius. Tessa and Marie-France out there on the ice, playing with movement."

Tessa and Scott were never fully satisfied with the final two segments of their short dance music, but Marie-France cut the tracks in such a way that they found the thread linking them all together fluidly. It actually became the more successful program, at least on the judging panels, throughout the season.

But the skaters' cherished work was the free dance, portraying the poignant, if doomed, relationship between the principal characters (played by Ewan McGregor and Nicole Kidman) in the grandiose and memorable 2001 movie *Moulin Rouge!* He was a Bohemian poet/author, she a courtesan who longed to be a legitimate actress but was oppressed by the cabaret owner and a

"WE PUT THE MUSIC ON AND IMMEDIATELY STARTED MOVING. THE CONNECTION WAS INSTANTANEOUS." —*Tessa*

Above and left: Tessa and Scott dance to "Long Time Running" by The Tragically Hip at the Skate Canada International in 2017. *Opposite: (above)* Practising for the 2017 Autumn Classic International; *(below)* performing their free dance at the Autumn Classic International.

Scott had seen the movie on late-night TV at home in Ilderton in April, when his grandfather was ill, and it made a huge impact on him.

"I felt something that I've felt very few times in my life," he recalls. "I thought, 'The person who made this is an artist. That's what we want to do: something artistically like that.' It can be a little bit weird, but it's so powerful, and anyone who was coming into the arena to watch us at the Olympic Games could relate to it."

He didn't think they'd end up with *Moulin Rouge!*, partly because a number of skaters had already used the music in the past, but he believed it was the best idea they'd had so far, and it established a benchmark. Anything that didn't

measure up to that feeling wouldn't be considered. "Because a big mistake in 2014 was that we didn't pick the right music," he explains.

They had also learned from 2014 that they couldn't please everybody, so from polling key people they trusted they framed a list of the critical components for Olympic music: it requires a crowd's reaction, people to be on their feet, or clapping along; it needs drama and power; and it should be something that's never been done before but is, at the same time, recognizable.

Scott was almost afraid to mention *Moulin Rouge!* to his partner, but while they were skating in Ilderton, he brought it up, "and it seemed to tick every one of those boxes," Tessa says. "We put the music on and immediately started moving. The connection was instantaneous. I still listen to it, and still love it."

Marie-France and Patrice didn't take to the idea. They believed it had been overdone, and didn't think *Moulin Rouge!* would enable Tessa and Scott to push the sport forward. But the skaters had a vision of how they could do it differently, and no other music was striking them so forcefully.

"When they see us move to it on the ice and see our enthusiasm, they start to come around, very slowly," Scott says, and Marie-France agreed to cut some music.

David Wilson was also involved with Marie-France in the choreography, but Tessa and Scott weren't quite sure that what they had in their minds could actually be done physically until off-ice dance coach Sam Chouinard suggested some pivotal movements.

"When we started working on those moves off ice, I actually had a moment where it was 'This is it. This is the stuff I've been dreaming about,'" Scott says.

They handily won their Grand Prix assignments at Skate Canada (where they set a new world record in the short dance) and NHK, while Gabriella and Guillaume did the same at Grand Prix stops in France and China (becoming the first dance team to break the 200-point barrier), and the Shibutanis won at Skate America and in Russia.

But during the fall Tessa and Scott struggled to land on a fitting energy balance for their free dance.

Scott had sometimes portrayed his character as too aggressively angry rather than jealous, and Tessa took a while to understand that during the "Roxanne" segment, her character should have a softer, more feminine energy than Scott's fiery intensity.

They received invaluable help from Cirque du Soleil acrobatic choreographer Silvia González in interpreting those nuances, and the multiple layers of storylines weaving through *Moulin Rouge!* Eventually they came to see that sometimes, especially in the beginning, the story didn't really involve the poet/author at all: it was all about the character development of the courtesan/actress. They used some

"WHEN WE STARTED WORKING ON THOSE MOVES OFF ICE, I ACTUALLY HAD A MOMENT WHERE IT WAS 'THIS IS IT. THIS IS THE STUFF I'VE BEEN DREAMING ABOUT.'"—*Scott*

Scott and Tessa came in at 199.86, and decided to take the huge risk of making major alterations with just two months left until the Olympics.

They estimate that they changed a full half of the free dance, but what the media focused on was a modification of their rotational lift, an ultra-sensual lift midway through the program. Tessa and Scott did that for technical reasons because it wasn't getting the marks it needed, not to make it more "family friendly," as was so widely believed.

Far more important was selecting a different edit from the *Moulin Rouge!* piece for the second segment of the free dance to provide more of a sustained love story, more of a duet, to finish strongly. Paradoxically, when they listen to the music on its own, they prefer their original haunting selections. "But you throw our skating into the mix," Tessa explains, "and there just wasn't enough time for the love story to evolve before this heartbreaking death. You felt kind of robbed. In the new version, you're into the pure love and joy quicker, then there's this major climax and it continues to end on a high, enveloping the audience. It's a big, major moment." Scott adds that with the triumphant feeling of the ending, the changes gave audiences their "Olympic moment," in which they want to jump to their feet.

And despite their worries to the contrary, it worked. They had never trained as hard as they did just before their two-day Christmas break, but the revamped free dance got sensational reviews in Vancouver, at the last Canadian championships of their career. That not only gave them an eighth senior title, but confidence and momentum heading into the Olympics, just as in 2010.

And between the short and free dances, they'd been asked by the Canadian Olympic Committee to be the flag-bearers at the opening ceremonies in Pyeongchang.

of the descriptors they'd applied to *Carmen* — raw, sensual, passionate, "dramatic with a twist" — and wanted a contemporary edge to their interpretation.

To separate their free dance from previous *Moulin Rouge!* programs, on certain beats of music they wanted to do exactly the opposite of what people might expect. It was an intriguing concept, and it's easy to see why they became so deeply invested in it. But while they had won both their Grand Prix assignments, their short dance was getting a more favourable reception than *Moulin Rouge!* They knew it would evolve with more training and competition and had already concluded that they needed more dramatic music at the end, but the entire team decided to wait to see how they did at the Grand Prix Final in Nagoya, Japan.

"We skated well there," Scott says. "Not amazingly, but we were very proud of it. But we lost."

Gabriella and Guillaume edged them by .53 points in the short dance, and took the free dance by 1.76 points to set a world record of 202.16 overall.

Above: Performing *Moulin Rouge!* at the Autumn Classic International. *Opposite (all photos):* Tessa and Scott visit Ottawa and meet with Prime Minister Justin Trudeau as he announces they will be Canada's flag-bearers at the Olympic opening ceremonies.

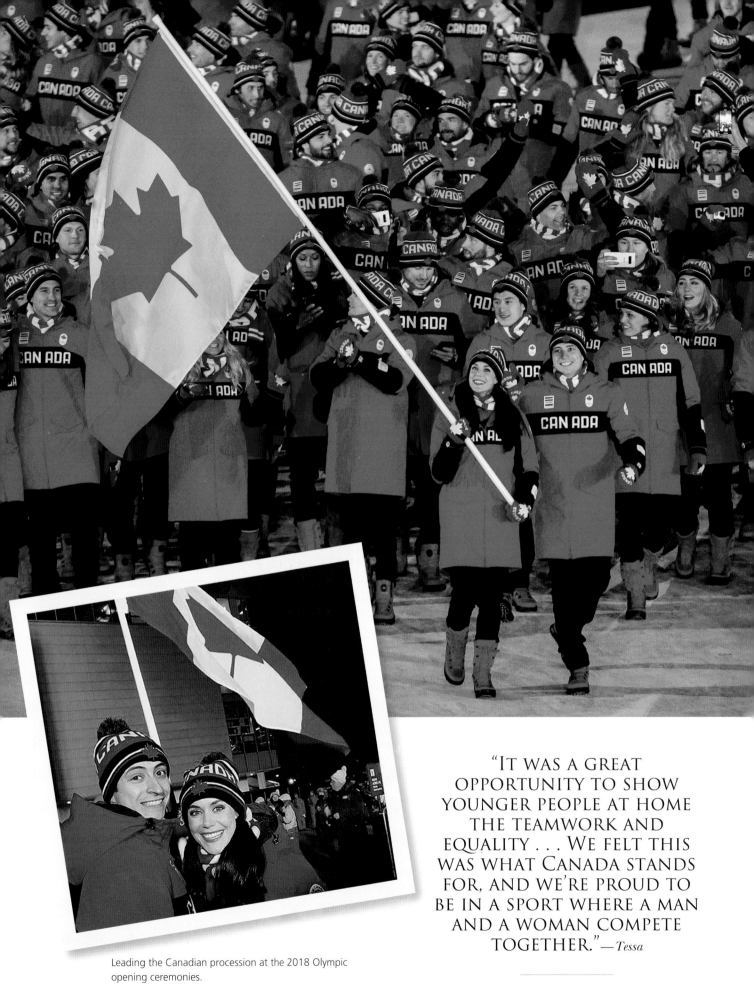

"IT WAS A GREAT
OPPORTUNITY TO SHOW
YOUNGER PEOPLE AT HOME
THE TEAMWORK AND
EQUALITY . . . WE FELT THIS
WAS WHAT CANADA STANDS
FOR, AND WE'RE PROUD TO
BE IN A SPORT WHERE A MAN
AND A WOMAN COMPETE
TOGETHER." —*Tessa*

Leading the Canadian procession at the 2018 Olympic
opening ceremonies.

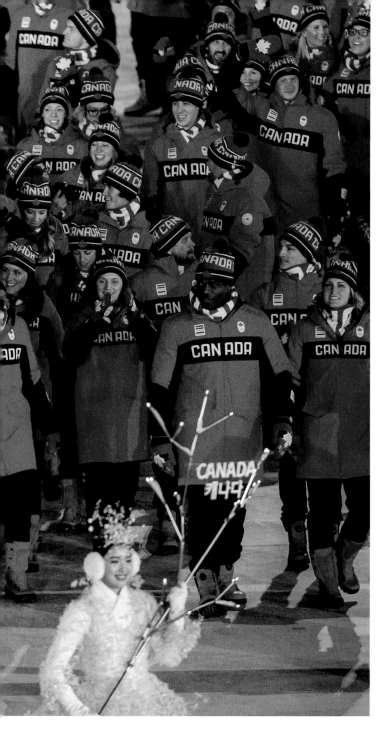

Canadians, and so they alternated carrying the flag, with Tessa first. At times they both had their hands on the flagpole. "It was a great opportunity to show younger people at home the teamwork and equality," Tessa explains. "We felt this was what Canada stands for, and we're proud to be in a sport where a man and a woman compete together." Scott says flag-bearing has its own singular place in their Olympic experiences.

With the opening ceremonies, Scott and Tessa were becoming Canada's favourite Olympic athletes. But they were also catching widespread international interest, particularly in the U.S., England, and Japan, because of their long history together, their longevity among the elite of their sport, their opportunity to become just the second ice dancers (after Oksana Grishuk and Evgeny Platov in 1994 and '98) to win two Olympic gold medals, and their compelling relationship and obvious chemistry. Thousands of tweeters, bloggers, television commentators, and news writers pined for them to be boyfriend and girlfriend, which they — still — are not.

But the mounting attention was lost on Tessa and Scott because the team skating event had begun that Friday and reconvened on Sunday. For months, the Canadian team had been determined to take gold, so they had strategized more than at the discipline's debut in Sochi, when they won silver. Gabriella and Guillaume had decided not to compete for France, but Tessa and Scott had committed to both the short and free dances because it gave Canada the best chance to win. They also relished the extra chance to perform their programs, and to get a feel for the Olympic ice and judging panels.

Patrick Chan might have underperformed in his short program, but he still fulfilled his assignment by beating the men from the U.S. and Russia, with Meagan Duhamel and Eric Radford finishing third in the pairs short and winning the free skate, and Kaetlyn Osmond third in the women's short. So Canada had a big lead, and significant momentum, heading into the final three skates on Monday. When Patrick Chan won the men's free skate, Canada had its gold. Gabrielle Daleman's solid third-place skate was icing on the cake, and

O**N FEBRUARY 9, 2018, A BITTERLY COLD** Friday night, Scott and Tessa marched into the Pyeongchang Olympic Stadium, carrying the red maple leaf, and followed by the rest of the 225-member Canadian Olympic team. Although they felt there were several other athletes who deserved to be flag-bearers, they were overwhelmed by the support and best wishes of the Canadian team. They had talked a lot about what message they wanted to convey to younger

During the team short dance at Pyeongchang. *Opposite: (above)* A first glimpse of the ice in Pyeongchang; *(below)* Team Canada cheers as Tessa and Scott take the ice during the team events.

J.-F. Ménard had never seen that side of them, so deeply "in the zone," and asked, incredulously, "What just happened?"

Tessa remembers thinking, "That's how you win the Olympics. I knew we were peaking and dialed in and I would not want to come up against us."

As they skated out to perform first in the final group of the short dance on Monday, February 19, Tessa had a small sense of foreboding, but drawing on all the mental preparation quickly transformed that into the mantra "We're unstoppable."

And they were. On the ice, Tessa sensed that there was something special about the performance, and indeed they broke their own world short dance record with a score of 83.67 points — putting some pressure on Gabriella and Guillaume, who were up next. Tessa and Scott had a little celebratory moment to themselves behind a backstage trailer, then casually emerged and said to J.-F. Ménard: "But we didn't come to the Olympics to win the short dance."

They didn't see much of their training mates' performance, including Gabriella's infamous wardrobe malfunction, but they did see some technical mistakes, and were mildly surprised at

Tessa and Scott had the surreal experience of riding the shuttle to the arena, knowing they were already guaranteed another Olympic gold medal. The vast TV audience assumed Tessa and Scott's free dance didn't matter, but to them it did, in a big way. They simulated how they would feel in the individual event, and, Scott says, "that made it easier when we stepped into that same position a week later."

Between the team and individual events, Scott and Tessa went to Seoul for three days, the first of which was spent mostly sleeping. During the next two days of practice they distanced themselves from the Games with the help of mental prep coach J.-F. Ménard. And they worked on improving the lower levels they'd received for some elements in the team event. They improved their transitions, changed the exit of a spin, fixed their choctaws, and reinstituted their original rotational lift, the so-called "sexy" one.

W ITH THE REFRESHING BOOST OF being away from twenty-four-hour Olympic fever, they were "lights out" in their first free dance practice back in Pyeongchang, revealing an elevated version of what they'd done in the team event to the judges, all of whom were in the practice rink.

some of the French team's grades of execution. The margin of victory was 1.7 points — much narrower than Canadian observers, particularly some vocal members of the Canadian media, felt was justified. There had been much widespread discussion in the world media during and before the Olympics about judging bias, as well as home-country favouritism (which didn't exclude criticism of Canadian judging), and the controversy bubbled again after the short dance. Kate Virtue and Alma Moir wondered if they might be looking at a situation similar to that of Sochi, but their children were thinking only of the free dance the next day.

They drew the number twenty position in the reduced roster of twenty couples, so appropriate for the last program of their competitive career, and Scott reminded Tessa that they had got exactly what they had always envisioned: holding a lead, and skating last.

So, on February 20, two years to the day after they announced their return to competition, Tessa

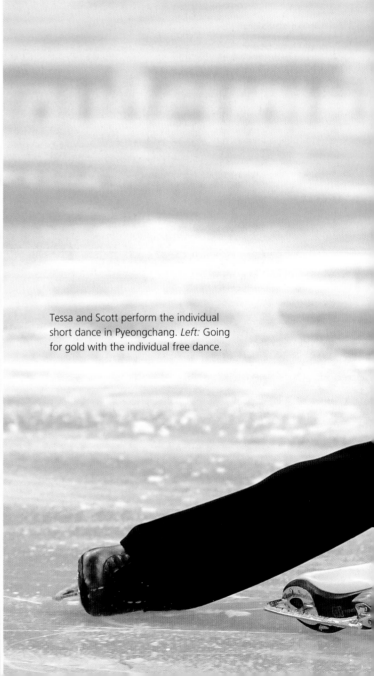

Tessa and Scott perform the individual short dance in Pyeongchang. *Left:* Going for gold with the individual free dance.

"IT WAS MAGICAL, THE FEELING IN THE ARENA WAS INCREDIBLE, THE CROWD REACTION WAS AMAZING." —*Alma Moir*

All photos: Tessa and Scott perform their gold medal–winning individual free dance in Pyeongchang.

and Scott did their warm-up for the free dance. They then had forty-five minutes to wait their turn, during which time Scott said, "This is exactly the story we want. We want all of the pressure."

Jean-François Ménard had mentioned that a lot of people would have empathy for Gabriella and Guillaume after their problems the previous day, and Tessa and Scott replied that they too felt badly for them: "They're friends." But J.-F. cautioned that they could not dwell on that. He also asked if they wanted to know how the French team had skated. Tessa and Scott replied that they'd just assume Gabriella and Guillaume would have the performance of their lives, then strive to skate to their own highest level. So they didn't know that their most formidable rivals had broken the world free dance record, with four points more than Scott and Tessa had ever recorded, and established a new total points standard of 205.28.

As Tessa and Scott skated to their starting positions at centre ice, some ten metres apart from each other, each emphatically crossing left foot over right, their families and friends sat riveted in the stands. In good seats behind the judges' table, Kate Virtue was holding the hand of her other daughter, Jordan. Two couples earlier they had seen the French skate brilliantly, and Kate worried about Scott and Tessa's chances, but Jordan assured her they could win. Beside them sat Alma and Joe Moir. They were joined for the final flight by their other two sons, Danny and Charlie, who'd found adjacent empty seats. Across the arena were nine other Moir family members and friends, including Carol and Paul Moir and their youngest daughter Cara. "So we had stereo sound," Alma laughs.

Alma Moir usually gauges whether to be nervous by the practice skate, and "they had a great practice." And once Tessa and Scott started skating, "they looked so confident, I had the same feeling I had in Vancouver. It was magical, the feeling in the arena was incredible, the crowd reaction was amazing."

Down on the ice, Tessa was looking into Scott's eyes and saying, "Let's do this." Scott was thinking that the first thirty seconds would be the most important, and that if he controlled the blade flow and knee action, once their bodies were working together, it would become a matter of focusing on each ten-second segment.

"I THINK I JUST SHOOK MY HEAD IN DISBELIEF." —*Tessa*

Celebrating on the ice, moments after the individual free dance.

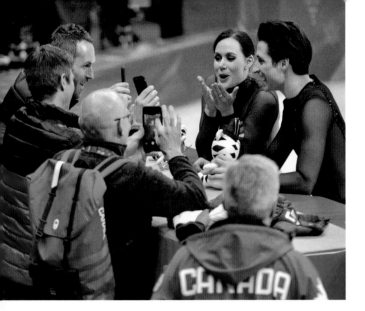

When the *Moulin Rouge!* music started, they didn't move for about five seconds, staring at — almost through — each other. They were building tension, setting a palpable tone of burning, dark passion. Slowly they started stroking, in a purposeful circle, almost like two animals of prey gauging each other. Then Tessa pivoted and leapt blindly backwards, locking onto Scott's hips, like a puppet being tugged by its strings. And it was on: the culmination of two years of laser-like focus. Forceful, dramatic movements during the strongest music, supple, sensitive strokes during the softest. Swift changes of edges, subtle tweaks of the largest muscles and smallest extremities. Indescribable unison and magnetism.

You try to fight it, Scott says, repeating his partner's belief "that feelings on the ice lie," but there are times when athletes can't help sensing they're "on the verge of skating out of your skin." And this was one of those times. They could feel the momentum swelling in the crowd, beginning with an audible stir after their twizzles.

"It started to come up and up and up and as we got closer to the ending, the electricity in the building just started to go through the roof," Tessa recalls.

On the "sexy" rotational lift, the crowd went crazy, as had happened in previous competitions. The audience exploded again on the final act of acclamation — which hadn't happened before — as Tessa balanced one skate on each of Scott's thighs, her arms outstretched and bent at the elbows in a universal pantomime of the torturous agony and ecstasy of love. And as the restructured music built to its last climax, a finale both triumphant

and tragic, Scott's arms thrust through the lift as a dramatic exclamation mark: not only to the *Moulin Rouge!* story they had just told, but to their own twenty-year story.

They had promised themselves that they wouldn't break the final positon or storyline as Scott's heartbroken character held the lifeless body of Tessa's character in his arms.

When they emerged from the hold, Scott said, "It was disbelief, almost. It's what we dreamed about, the fact that we made it happen that well."

"I think I just shook my head in disbelief," Tessa says pensively.

They hugged, almost desperately, she on the edge of laughter, he on the edge of crying into her right shoulder, abandoning themselves to happiness, relief, and the opinions of nine judges. Then they slowly backed away from each other, which they do not remember doing, one's eyes never leaving the other's. Tessa pulled her hands to her face, in incredulous joy, staring over her fingertips at Scott, who was now pumping his arms like a hockey player who'd scored the biggest goal of his career. The scene was, as those who know Scott and Tessa understood, *so them.*

Tessa says she was watching Scott's surge of pure adrenalin, feeling so happy for him, as he was feeling for her.

"That moment you have on the ice together, before you get feedback from the judges and coaches, before you hear from the fans, is always the most important to us," Scott says. "And we would have stayed out there forever if we could."

In the kiss and cry, the free dance scores indicated that they had finished a close second in the segment to Gabriella and Guillaume. And

Above: Receiving their free dance scores, and a celebratory hug. *Below:* An emotional moment with coaches Patrice and Marie-France. *Opposite:* (above) On the ice following their gold medal–winning performance, Tessa and Scott celebrate with members of the B2ten team in person and via video call; (below) with Patrice, J.-F., and Marie-France in the kiss and cry.

then the total scores came up: they had set a new world record of 206.07 points, enough to win by just eight-tenths of a point.

When they realized it, Scott slapped his knee and jumped as if propelled from a slingshot, and Tessa threw her head forward into her hands. He lifted her again and set her down for a quick kiss and another prolonged hug. Before joining in, Marie-France and Patrice sat smiling on either side of them, allowing Tessa and Scott those few precious seconds to celebrate — despite millions of onlookers — on their own.

In the stands, the other Virtues and Moirs were hugging and yelling, "They did it! They did it!" Carol Moir, having trouble dividing her favourite-aunt relationship with Scott from the first-coach relationship, was watching Tessa with massive pride, seeing "someone you've helped start reach the highest you can reach in our sport."

At home in his Waterloo condo with his wife Carolyn Allwright, their second coach, Paul MacIntosh — having eaten his competition day club sandwich and sent his traditional "Be the class of the ice" e-mail — was also beaming. "They had four unbelievable performances and it kept building, each one better than the one before," he says.

When Tessa and Scott left the kiss and cry, they ducked between a curtain and a door to have a quiet moment alone, remembering all they'd been through. They knew it was the end and didn't speak much, because it was difficult to even form a sentence. "We just hugged and looked at each other," Tessa says. "We knew what each other was thinking."

They both say that's the moment they will remember forever.

And then, Scott recalls quietly, "We opened the door, to share ourselves with the rest of the world."

"SCOTT AS AN ATHLETE
IS UNMATCHED
IN EVERY WAY:
HIS DRIVE, HIS PASSION,
HIS COMMITMENT
TO EXCELLENCE, AND
HIS RELENTLESS PURSUIT
FOR PERFECTION IS
WHAT SETS HIM APART." —*Tessa*

"I'VE BEEN IN AWE FOR
TWENTY-ONE YEARS, SINCE
THIS LITTLE GIRL WALKED
INTO MY LIFE AND
CHANGED IT FOREVER. IT'S
PRETTY AMAZING TO LOOK
BACK AND HAVE SHARED
SO MUCH." —*Scott*

Posing with their gold medals at the 2018 Pyeongchang Olympics. *Opposite*: Tessa and Scott with coaches Patrice Lauzon (*left*) and Marie-France Dubreuil (*right*) before the Olympic Opening Ceremonies.

Chapter Eight

TRUE PARTNERS

TESSA AND SCOTT LOOK BACK ON THEIR TWENTY-YEAR PARTNERSHIP AND TURN THEIR ATTENTION TO THE FUTURE.

W HEN THEY STEPPED THROUGH that backstage door and into the awaiting sea of Olympic television rights-holders, then radio rights-holders, and then the bulging print media mob, Scott and Tessa did so as the most decorated Olympic figure skaters of all time.

That 0.79-point margin of difference between them and their friends Gabriella Papadakis and Guillaume Cizeron had elevated them to a third Olympic figure skating gold medal, tied with a trio of transcendent athletes: Sweden's early pioneer, Gillis Grafström; Norway's Sonja Henie, the woman credited with initiating North America's enduring love of figure skating; and the incomparable Russian pairs skater Irina Rodnina. These three icons are also the only skaters to have done what Tessa and Scott had just done: win an Olympic gold

medal eight years after they won their first one, an indication of unfathomable perseverance at the top of their field. With two more chances than most previous Olympians as competitors in the team event, Tessa and Scott are the only figure skaters to have won five Olympic medals: three gold and two silver.

Their list of statistical accomplishments is extraordinarily lengthy: they set the world record for the free dance three times, for the short dance eight times, and for total points seven times, including on the very last day of their competitive career. They were the first skaters to receive a perfect 10.0 under the revamped ISU scoring system, the youngest ice dancers and first team from North America to win Olympic gold, and the first world junior champions to win the Olympics with the same partnership. And it goes on and on.

Plus, they were the first duo ever to carry the Canadian flag into an Olympic opening ceremony.

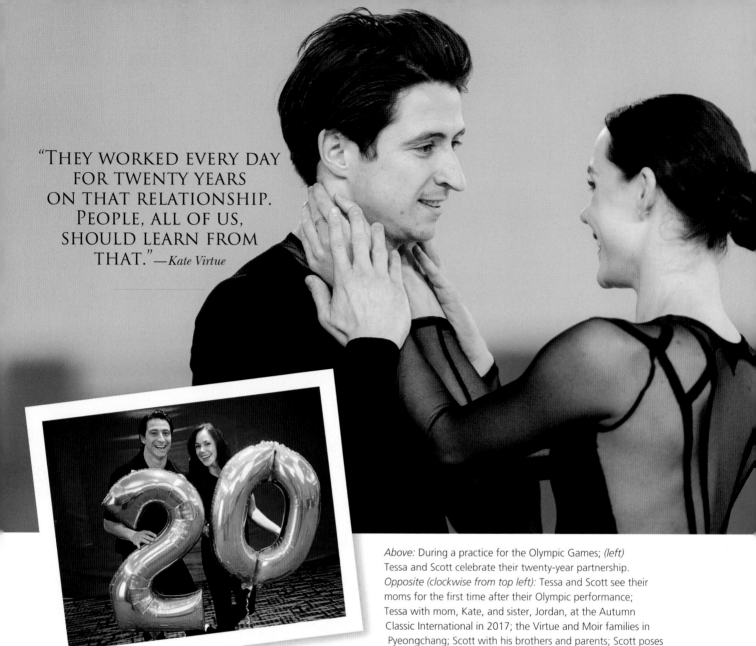

"THEY WORKED EVERY DAY
FOR TWENTY YEARS
ON THAT RELATIONSHIP.
PEOPLE, ALL OF US,
SHOULD LEARN FROM
THAT." —*Kate Virtue*

Above: During a practice for the Olympic Games; *(left)* Tessa and Scott celebrate their twenty-year partnership. *Opposite (clockwise from top left):* Tessa and Scott see their moms for the first time after their Olympic performance; Tessa with mom, Kate, and sister, Jordan, at the Autumn Classic International in 2017; the Virtue and Moir families in Pyeongchang; Scott with his brothers and parents; Scott poses with mom, Alma *(left), and* aunt Carol *(right)*.

But it wasn't only their tangible achievements that had made them the face of the 2018 Canadian Olympic team and boosted them from national praise and adoration to far wider, international acclaim.

They were beloved by international broadcasters, on social media, and in all forms of cyberspace. There was boundless, incessant analysis of, and opinions about, their relationship — a palpable collective wish, if not supposition, that they were in real life what they so often portrayed on ice: a deeply involved romantic couple. Tessa has said repeatedly that, while not true, that assumption is the greatest compliment they could ever receive on their artistry.

"They kind of became the North American sweethearts," says their early coach Paul MacIntosh. "It's such a good story: the intrigue of their relationship, and just the length of it, how they started out as such young kids."

Kate Virtue adds: "They worked every day for twenty years on that relationship. People, all of us, should learn from that."

The millions of people around the world who follow figure skating, even the harshest critics among them, recognize the broad variety of theme, style, tempo, and athleticism Tessa and Scott have brought to their discipline over their many years at or near the top. They were neither just superior athletes, nor just superior artists, but the

Left and opposite: Tessa and Scott perform their "Long Time Running" routine for the Olympic Figure Skating Gala in 2018.

personification of the almost invisible marriage of both — constantly blurring the lines of the duality that has defined skating for more than a century.

They helped make their sport "cool." Alexei Yagudin, the 2002 Olympic men's champion, once told Tessa and Scott he never watched ice dancing until they came along.

And when they returned to competitive skating after two years, during which it was evolving possibly more quickly than ever, they succeeded beyond anyone's expectations. In their two-year return they won eleven of their twelve competitions. In the previous ninety years of the sport, only one other skater (Jan Hoffmann in 1980) had ever won a world title five years after winning the previous one.

Their Comeback became a classic and multi-level storyline all on its own, underscored by their younger, ascendant rivals who, in an encore of previous Olympics, were also training partners. Their repeatedly emphasized reasons for returning to competitive skating — to finish the unfinished, to better themselves as skaters and people while advancing ice dancing in the process — resonated with the broader Olympic-period audience. And it was clear that they were enjoying it, no matter how difficult it sometimes was behind the scenes.

"Those last two years brought their love of the sport back to them," Alma Moir says.

And everyone could see it.

It was against this intense and emotional backdrop that Tessa and Scott began their farewell to the competitive skating scene, which would be formally announced in the fall of 2018.

As usual after an Olympic skating event ends, and especially with a widely popular victory, there was a heavy media gauntlet to run that would take up most of the rest of gold medal day and the next day, too, up at Pyeongchang's mountain studios. But in between, Tessa and Scott got to spend fifteen minutes with their families at Canada House.

"It was very emotional," Tessa recalls. "I cried a lot. It was about pure happiness."

Scott says that he can remember the first moment in every Olympics that he saw his family after he and Tessa had finished skating. They have always been aware of, and thankful for, how much their parents and siblings have sacrificed for their skating careers: the costs involved; taking vacations to coincide with competition; spending so much time in arena lobbies and practice rinks talking skating; being supportive without pressuring; and emphasizing that they do things the right way, with

Above and opposite: Fans greet Tessa and Scott at the London, Ontario, airport as they return home from Pyeongchang.
Right: (top and bottom) The Arkells perform at Canada House in Pyeongchang as Tessa looks on with friends Allie Grand and Kat Bitove.

core values that they carried not only in victory, but through defeat. So it was always important to share that moment with them.

And they're proud of how, in a sport whose partnerships are often ended by parental conflict, their own parents got along so well with each other.

"We've been paired up for twenty years together, but our families have too," Tessa says. "We're very lucky they got along so well together."

Scott adds, "Kate would never have let anybody say anything bad about me in any lobby in any rink that she ever stood in . . . and it was the same with Alma about Tessa."

Kate Virtue says that during the last Olympic year she often felt "how lucky we were to have had twenty fabulous years with the Moirs. I wouldn't have wanted to have spent it with anyone else. It's been the best partnership on all levels."

After the media crush, Tessa and Scott settled into enjoying the Games and supporting their Canadian teammates at as many events as they could. Scott spent time with two lifelong friends, Matt Ward and Brad Funston, who had flown to South Korea.

They also skated in the traditional gala which ends most skating events, performing a tribute to the late Gord Downie and the Tragically Hip. They had been inspired all season by Downie's the Arkells saw a video showing Canadian athletes belting it out at Canada House, they tweeted that they had to be there in person to play that song for the team. In what Tessa calls "a really great social media story," Air Canada immediately tweeted that the airline could make it happen, and had them in South Korea two days later for two memorable performances at Canada House.

Returning from Pyeongchang, Tessa and Scott were physically depleted, as are so many athletes, in the aftermath period often referred to as the post-Olympic blues. They took a week away from media interviews for the first week home in Canada, but were soon back into a chaotic schedule that left them no room to fully process what they had just gone through, or what might lie ahead. They were not ungrateful for the attention, but it was exhausting, and their calendar was full, every day, right into December. Scott says it can often take eight months for Olympic athletes to get their feet fully back under them: "It's hard enough at twenty-eight and thirty; I don't know we ever did it at twenty and twenty-two."

As a reflection of their enormous international popularity, fans of *The Ellen DeGeneres Show* lobbied producers to invite Tessa and Scott into NBC's Burbank, California, studio. Ellen, always the comedienne, pestered them constantly about their relationship and refused to accept that they weren't a romantic couple.

Back home, they made a series of appearances on shows like CTV's *The Social*. "The Canadian market for us is so special," Scott explains. "To walk into the studio and have people going so crazy. People in Canada were a part of at least ten years of this. We were so lucky to have our story be followed and have people identify with us: they were a huge part of it. They've seen the victories and the defeats and the rising to the occasion in Pyeongchang."

They love working closely with their sponsors and accepting speaking engagements which are more like conversations: events at that they can tell their story, be open and honest about what they think, and encourage young people to pursue their dreams fearlessly.

They have committed to the skating partnership through 2019, and will then reassess.

ability to make the audience feel deeply and by how the band, knowing Downie was dying, had crossed the country to share their music with Canadians one last time. He and Tessa had choreographed "Long Time Running" themselves for the 2017 Skate Canada gala, a few days after Downie died, thinking it would be a one-off, but Marie-France suggested they "take it and run with it."

In their careers, Tessa and Scott have often skated show programs to Canadian music, and "Long Time Running" obviously made sense for a team that's been together for twenty years.

"There are a lot of people across the world who don't know the Tragically Hip story," Scott says. "Maybe some of our Russian fans now will listen to the Hip. It's super-Canadian."

And so is another important Canadian band, the Arkells, "good Hamilton boys," as Scott calls them. During their normal "blackout" period before the Games, he and Tessa had agreed to do a video promotion for the Arkells' 2018 stadium show, which was announced on the day of the opening ceremonies. During the Games, the band's "Knocking at the Door" became an unofficial anthem for the entire Canadian team, and when

"WE WERE SO LUCKY
TO HAVE OUR STORY
BE FOLLOWED
AND HAVE PEOPLE
IDENTIFY WITH US." —*Scott*

"We might continue after that, but we don't know for certain," Tessa says honestly. "We have an idea of what we want to achieve with our pro career, and while working as touring skaters, as we did in 2014 and '15, is great, we can't live like that for long. We're interested in pursuing different projects and new opportunities to find fulfillment."

One of their major projects is mounting their own "Thank You, Canada" tour in the fall of 2018. With a supporting cast of Canadian contemporaries, Tessa and Scott plan to visit thirty smaller municipalities across the country. "Visiting towns and cities that don't normally get major skating productions is important to us," says Tessa. "It's our opportunity to give back to our grassroots fan base."

Scott likes to point out that while he is always considered the partner with the sense of humour, "and the one to make a stupid joke, Tessa really is the funny one, and she's made me laugh for so many years."

That, in turn, leads Tessa to observe that it's a truism that when someone you respect thinks you're funny, or smart, or brave, you find yourself being funny, or smart, or brave.

And when they are asked to describe each other, both say that there would never be enough time to get it exactly right.

"I don't have the superlatives in my vocabulary to describe Scott," Tessa says, speaking first. "I think in all of this discussion about what our partnership means, we're the two people, right in the centre of it, who understand the least about it because it's all we know. So it's hard to have that

Above: Tessa and Scott join the hosts of CTV's *The Social.*
Opposite: Tessa and Scott pose in front of the artist entry at *The Ellen DeGeneres Show.*

"I THINK IN ALL OF
THIS DISCUSSION ABOUT
WHAT OUR PARTNERSHIP MEANS,
WE'RE THE TWO PEOPLE,
RIGHT IN THE CENTRE OF IT,
WHO UNDERSTAND THE LEAST
ABOUT IT BECAUSE
IT'S ALL WE KNOW." —*Tessa*

Above: Scott and Tessa share a moment at practice during the Autumn Classic International. *Opposite (clockwise from left):* Behind the scenes at a media event at Canada House in Pyeongchang; Tessa and Scott meet retired astronaut Cmdr. Chris Hadfield; Tessa and Scott pose with Drake after a Toronto Raptors game.

perspective on it. It's unique, and we cherish that because we know we are so lucky to have found each other and to be able to work together. We've worked so hard at it. We're kind of an extension of one another at this point.

"I think Scott as an athlete is unmatched in every way: his drive, his passion, his commitment to excellence, and his relentless pursuit for perfection is what sets him apart. Add to that this organic natural flair for pure emotion and raw passion. Seeing him move is so interesting because it just comes from within, from this place where you can't imagine him doing anything else. And you can't teach that. We worked on it for twenty years, but you can't teach the glide of the blade that he has. It's unlike anyone else's.

"He's also the most generous person: generous with his time, generous with his heart, generous with his thoughtfulness. He just gives so much."

After characteristically joking how difficult it is to have to follow Tessa's thoughts, Scott says, "When I think about our partnership I just think about how fortunate I have been right from the start. I've been in awe for twenty-one years, since this little girl walked into my life and changed it forever. It's pretty amazing to look back and have shared so much and still go into the rink and only care — above and beyond anything else — what she thinks. It's so hard to put into words, but I wish people got to see more of what I got to see for twenty years: the way she can move to any

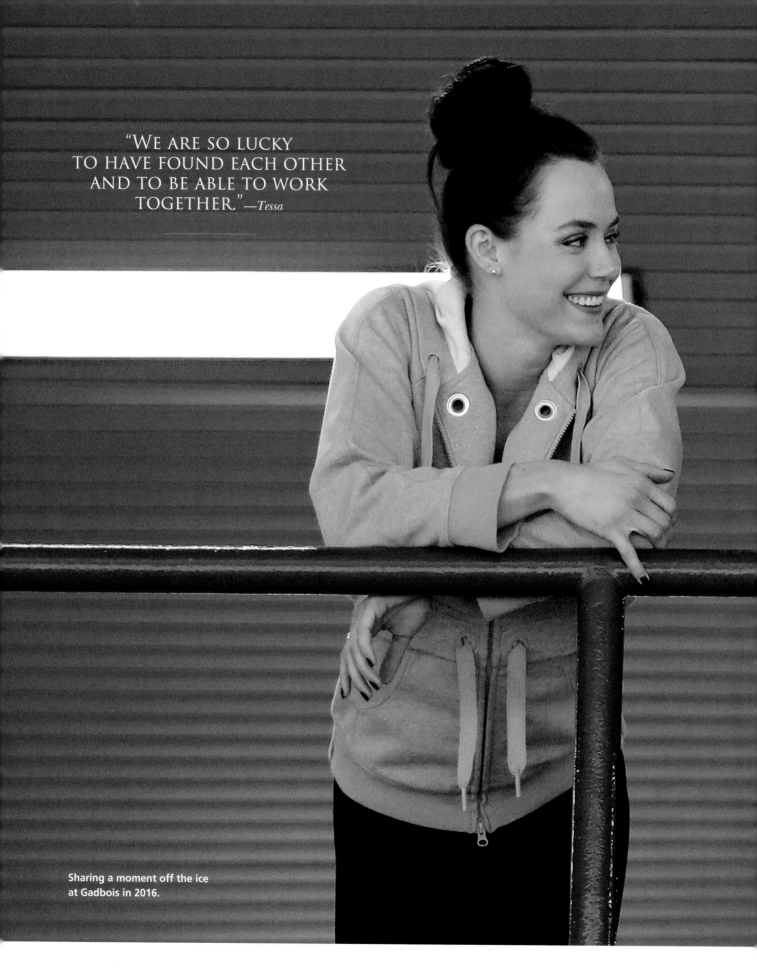

"WE ARE SO LUCKY TO HAVE FOUND EACH OTHER AND TO BE ABLE TO WORK TOGETHER." —*Tessa*

Sharing a moment off the ice at Gadbois in 2016.

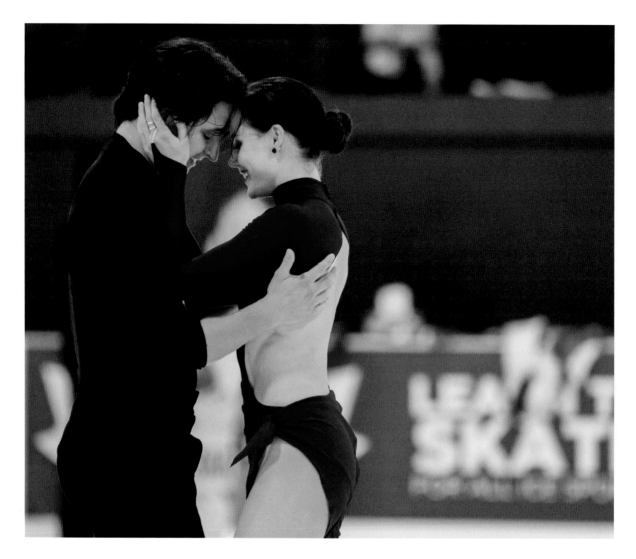

Above: Scott and Tessa perform at the 2017 Autumn Classic International in Montreal.
Opposite: On the ice at the 2018 Pyeongchang Olympics.

music. I've never seen it in any professional that I've worked with, and I've worked with the best.

"I love her drive, her fierce competitiveness, the athlete I've seen just continue to develop. It's pretty crazy to be an Olympic champion at twenty and not even be scratching the surface of how fierce an athlete you can be. For the last little bit of this, I was terrified just trying to keep up.

"But it's the personal side that you have to understand. People can see my fire and my emotion, but that's not easy to work with. I don't hold any of it back. You need someone who really is consistent, day in and day out, and that's Tess. I can't think of too many times in her life when she has

come out to the rink and been unreasonable. But at the same time, she carries these emotions, tells these stories. It really is amazing and I still don't know how it works.

"We have the best times together and our business relationship is next to none. If we were a Fortune 500 company I wouldn't want to come up against us. We work together so well.

"Tessa says it's caring more for each other than you care about yourself, and she's right."

"Maybe, at the root of it, that's what we have more than anything else, that we really care about each other," Tessa concludes.

"And that's really special."

"At the end of this all it would be really nice if we were just remembered for being ourselves." —*Tessa*

PHOTOGRAPHY CREDITS

Every reasonable effort has been made to trace ownership of copyright materials. The publisher will gladly rectify any inadvertent errors or omissions in credits in future editions.

CP IMAGES

Mike Ridewood, 2, 137 (top)
AP Photo/David Zalubowski, 72
Andrew Vaughan, 73
Paul Chiasson, 77, 91, 93, 94–95, 105, 109, 110–111, 115, 128–29, 144, 145, 172
AP Photo/Lee Jin-Man, 78, 83 (top), 85

AP Photo/Itsuo Inouye, 81
AP Photo/Junji Jurokawa, 100, 112–113
Darryl Dyck, 102, 106–107
Mark Spowart, 124
AP Photo/Ivan Sekretarev, 133
Robert Skinner, 134

The Canadian Press/Geoff Robins, 140 (bottom), 141, 222 (all photos), 223 (top left)
The Canadian Press/Dave Chidley, 149
The Canadian Press/Bernat Armangue, 171

DANIELLE EARL/GOLDEN SKATE

v; 187 (left); 189 (bottom); 196 (bottom); 200–201; 204 (left); 206 (all photos); 207 (all photos); 211 (top left); 213; 218 (top); 220; 230; 236

GETTY IMAGES

Matthew Stockman, vi, 173 (top left)
Kevork Djansezian, xxi
Chung Sung-Jun, 82
Jamie McDonald, 86
AFP Photo/Mark Ralston, 97 (bottom)

AFP Saeed Khan, 122–123
Jasper Juinen/Getty Images, 126, 130–131
AFP Photo Yuri Kadobnov, 127, 129 (right)
AFP Dimitar Dilkoff, 136

Clive Rose, 142–143
Oleg Nikishin, 157 (bottom right)
Paul Gilham, 168 (bottom left)
Clive Mason, 170

MYRA KLARMAN

76; 88 (right); 89; 154; 155

GREG KOLZ/SKATE CANADA

x; 150; 160; 161; 162–163 (all photos); 176; 180 (top); 181; 182 (bottom); 186 (all photos); 188; 190 (bottom); 192–193 (all photos); 194 (all photos); 195 (all photos); 197 (all photos); 198; 202; 203 (bottom); 204–205; 211 (top right); 216; 219 (top right and middle); 221; 227; 228–229; 239

ALMA MOIR

8 (all photos); 9 (all photos, bottom left photo c/o Cedar Lane Studios); 10; 12 (bottom right); 13; 16; 17 (top left); 83 (bottom); 118 (bottom left); 138 (centre left)

CARA MOIR

191 (all photos); 219 (bottom left and bottom right)

ELINA PAASONEN

ii–iii; 157 (top); 159 (all photos); 164; 165; 167; 182–183; 184; 187 (right);
189 (top); 190 (top); 208–209; 212; 231

KATE VIRTUE

5 (all photos); 6 (all photos); 11 (all photos); 12 (top left); 14 (all photos); 17 (right and bottom left); 18; 19; 22; 23; 24 (all photos); 25; 27 (all photos); 28; 29 (all photos); 30 (all photos); 31; 32; 33; 34; 35 (all photos); 36; 37; 38–39 (all photos); 40 (all photos); 41; 44; 45; 46; 47 (all photos); 48; 49; 50-51; 52; 53; 54 (all photos); 55 (all photos); 56; 58; 59 (all photos); 60; 61; 62 (all photos); 63; 64 (all photos); 66 (all photos); 67; 70; 71; 74; 75; 79; 80; 84 (all photos); 87; 88 (left); 90; 92; 97 (top); 104; 111 (right); 116–117 (all photos); 118–119; 120; 121 (all photos); 135 (top and bottom right); 137 (bottom); 138 (top, bottom, and centre right); 139 (all photos); 140 (top); 152–153

TESSA VIRTUE

158; 169; 173 (top right); 180 (bottom); 185 (all photos); 199 (top right); 200 (bottom);
203 (top); 217; 218 (left); 219 (top left); 223 (top right and bottom), 224; 226 (all photos)

Image on page xvii © Johany Jutras
Image on page 135 (bottom left) © Rick Madonik
Image on page 148 © Zoe Alexopoulos, FloFoto
Image on page 153 (bottom right) © Sport Korea
Image on page 153 (top right) © Cylla Von Tiedemann
Image on page 166 © Alamy/Aflo Co. Ltd.
Image on page 168 © Anya Chibis
Image on page 179 © Chris Robart
Image on page 196 (top) © Danielle Earl/Skate Canada
Image on page 199 (top left and bottom) © Adam Scotti, Prime Minister's Office
Image on pages 210 (all photos) © Aoran Liu
Image on page 211 (bottom right) © Tianyuan Zhang
Image on page 225 © CTV/Mark O'Neill

ACKNOWLEDGEMENTS

Thank you to our fabulous, loving families, who have not only provided unconditional love and support, but also sacrificed immensely and encouraged us to go after our dreams. You've kept us grounded and served as our perfect "safe place" throughout this rollercoaster of a journey.

To those Canadian ice dancers that came before us — Tracy Wilson and Rob McCall, Shae-Lynn Bourne and Victor Kraatz, Megan Wing and Aaron Lowe, and Marie-France Dubreuil and Patrice Lauzon — thank you for paving the way. Your creativity, work ethic, and class were inspirational. Thanks for showing us that anything is possible.

Our journey started at the Ilderton Skating Club and has included a magnificent cast of professionals who helped launch our career. Thanks so much to Carol Moir, Paul MacIntosh, Suzanne Killing-Wood, and Rebecca Babb, who gave us excellent basic skating skills and shaped our approach to training, competing, and relating to one another. They taught us many lessons that reach far beyond the boards of a rink and made us strive to be the "class of the ice." To Marina Zoueva, Igor Shpilband, and Johnny Johns for their vision, dedication, and focus. They contributed to our knowledge of technique and challenged us to find our own signature style. Thanks to Mary Brannagan, Maria Mountain, Brian Gastaldi, and Earl Wenk — the support team that helped us through the bulk of our career with steadfast commitment and unwavering encouragement.

There are no words to properly express our gratitude for Marie-France Dubreuil, Patrice Lauzon, Roman Hagenauer, and Sam Chouinard. Thank you for your love, passion, unparalleled wisdom, collaborative spirit, and belief in us. You gave us wings.

Profound thanks to our B2ten team, including Dominick Gauthier, JD Miller, Dave Campbell, Jaime and Scotty Livingston,

Jean François Menard, Chris Rozdilsky, John Flood, Ann McMillan, Kimberly Wong, Kim McQueen, and Alexia de Macar, without whom we could not have reached the top of the podium in Korea — your progressive approach to training, relentless pursuit of excellence, and ability to insulate us with support while offering us the autonomy we needed to forge our own path will never be forgotten. We love you guys and will forever cherish the bonds we have formed.

Thanks to Skate Canada for providing us with opportunities and experiences that reached a pinnacle in Pyeongchang. You gave us the tools and resources that ultimately helped us in handling the pressure of competition. Special thanks to Benoît Lavoie, Mike Slipchuk, Leanna Caron, and Debra Armstrong for your feedback, thoughtful insight, and advice — much love and hugs.

A heartfelt thanks to Steve Milton, for whom we have the utmost respect, and who helped us tell our story and made the process most enjoyable.

And a huge thank you to our loyal fans who continually amaze and motivate us! Your support and cheers never go unnoticed.

— *Tessa and Scott*

Heartfelt thanks to my Inner Circle — Jess, Toby, Karen, Josh, and all the grandkids — for their love and vibrancy; to Laura for seeing me through; to Doug, Sarah, Maria, and the rest of the supportive House of Anansi group for their vision; to the Virtue and Moir families for their inclusiveness; and, as always, to Tessa and Scott, for being exactly who they are.

— *Steve Milton*

ABOUT THE AUTHORS

TESSA VIRTUE and **SCOTT MOIR** are the most decorated figure skaters in history, having won the Olympic gold medal for ice dance at the 2010 Vancouver Olympic Games, two silver medals at the 2014 Sochi Games, and two gold medals at the 2018 Pyeongchang Games. Additionally, in their twenty-one-year partnership, they have won four World Championships (three senior and one junior), three Four Continents Championships, nine Canadian Championships (eight senior and one junior), and six Skate Canada International titles. In a stunning performance at the 2018 Olympic Games, they recaptured the world record for highest total score in ice dancing.

STEVE MILTON has over forty years' experience as a sportswriter and writes for the *Hamilton Spectator*. He has won numerous Ontario Newspaper Awards and has been both a Gemini and National Newspaper Award finalist. He is the author of more than twenty books and is a member of both the Skate Canada Hall of Fame and the Canadian Football Hall of Fame. He lives in Hamilton, Ontario.